COLORADO
SNOW
CLIMBS

A GUIDE FOR ALL SEASONS

COLORADO SNOW CLIMBS

A GUIDE FOR ALL SEASONS

DAVE COOPER

The Colorado Mountain Club Press
Golden, Colorado

WARNING: Mountain climbing and hiking are high-risk activities. This guidebook is not a substitute for your experience and common sense. The users of this guideboook assume full responsibility for their own safety. Weather, terrain conditions, and individual technical abilities must be considered before undertaking any of the climbs and hikes in this guide. The Colorado Mountain Club and the author do not assume any liability for injury, damage to property, or violation of the law that may result from the use of this book.

PUBLISHED BY

The Colorado Mountain Club Press
710 Tenth Street, Suite 200, Golden, Colorado 80401
303-996-2743   e-mail: cmcpress@cmc.org
Founded in 1912, The Colorado Mountain Club is the largest outdoor recreation, education, and conservation organization in the Rocky Mountains. Look for our books at your local bookstore or outdoor retailer or online at www.cmc.org/books

Alan Bernhard—design and composition, Boulder Bookworks
John Gascoyne—proofreader
Dianne Nelson—copyeditor, Shadow Canyon Graphics
Alan Stark—publisher

DISTRIBUTED TO THE BOOK TRADE BY

Mountaineers Books
1001 SW Klickitat Way, Suite 201, Seattle, WA 98134, 800-533-4453

COVER IMAGE: Climber approaching the summit on Fletcher Mountain's southeast ridge. The couloir visible in the foreground is described in Route 23. Photo by Dave Cooper.

We gratefully acknowledge the financial support of the people of Colorado through the Scientific and Cultural Facilities District of greater metropolitan Denver for our publishing activities.

First Edition
ISBN 978-0-9760525-9-3

Printed in Canada

CONTENTS

WINTER INTO SPRING

SPRING INTO SUMMER

SUMMER

SUMMER INTO AUTUMN

SEASONAL SNOW CLIMBING GUIDE

	DEC	JAN	FEB	
WINTER INTO SPRING				
1. "Atlantic Peak"—West Ridge	■	■	■	
2. Fletcher Mountain via "Drift Peak"	■	■	■	
3. Grizzly Peak	■	■	■	
4. Byers Peak	■			
5. North Star Mountain—East Ridge	■	■	■	
6. Mount Bancroft—East Ridge	■	■	■	
7. Mount Lady Washington—Martha Couloir	■	■	■	
8. Longs Peak—North Face (Cables Route)	■	■	■	
9. Mount Guyot—Southeast Ridge				
10. Fletcher Mountain—Southeast Ridge				
SPRING INTO SUMMER				
11. Quandary Peak—South Couloir				
12. Wheeler Mountain				
13. Castle Peak—Northeast Ridge				
14. Niagara Peak—Northeast Face and East Ridge				
15. Flattop Mountain—Dragons Tail Couloir				
16. Torreys Peak—Dead Dog Couloir				
17. South Arapaho Peak—South Couloir				
18. Mount Jasper Snow Climbs				
19. Mount Neva—Northeast Cirque				
20. Savage Mountain—The Savage Couloir				
21. Mount Democrat—North Couloir				
22. Mount Meeker—Dreamweaver				
23. Fletcher Mountain—East Face Routes				
24. "Citadel Peak" Couloirs				
25. "East Thorn"—North Couloir				
26. Pacific Peak—North Couloir				
27. Snowdon Peak—Northwest Couloir				
28. Quandary Peak—North Face Couloirs				
29. Sundance Mountain—North Face Couloir				
30. Longs Peak Area—The Flying Dutchman Couloir				
SUMMER				
31. James Peak—Northeast Face Couloirs				
32. North Twilight Peak—North Face Couloirs				
33. Potosi Peak—North Couloir				
34. Longs Peak—Notch Couloir				
35. Ypsilon Mountain—East Face				
SUMMER INTO AUTUMN				
36. Flattop Mountain Couloirs—"Ptarmigan Fingers"				
37. Rollins Pass Area—Challenger Glacier				
38. Rollins Pass Area—Skyscraper Glacier				
39. Apache Peak—Fair Glacier and Queens Way Couloir				
40. Taylor Glacier				
41. Tyndall Glacier				
42. Thatchtop—Powell Ice Field				

	MAR	APR	MAY	JUN	JUL	AUG	SEP	OCT	NOV

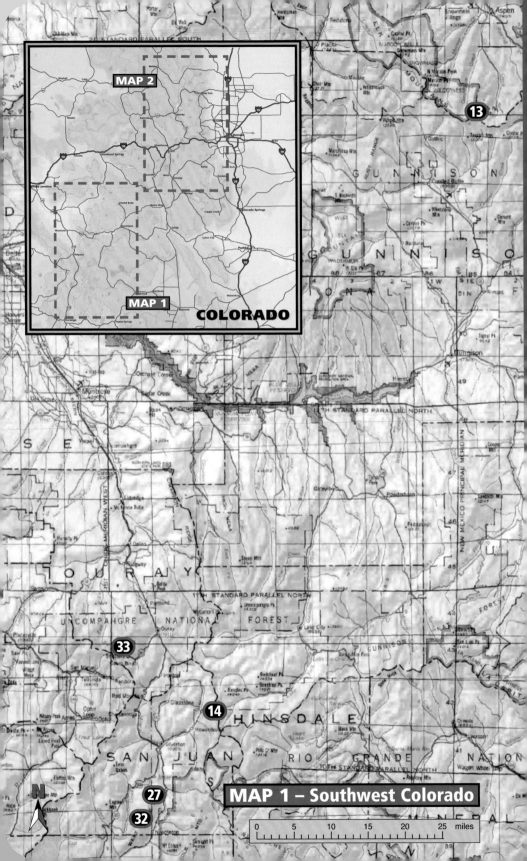

MAP 2

MAP 1

COLORADO

MAP 1 – Southwest Colorado

0   5   10   15   20   25   miles

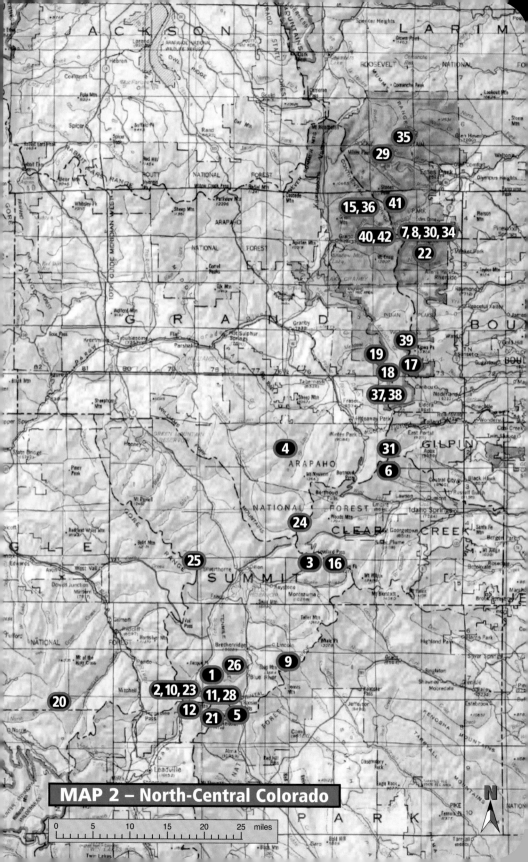

MAP 2 – North-Central Colorado

0   5   10   15   20   25   miles

N

ACKNOWLEDGMENTS

This book would not have happened without the help and support of many friends who have joined me on the climbs over the years; sometimes, I suspect, putting aside their own goals to help with this project. I would like to thank Jean Aschenbrenner, Trace Baker, Dan Bereck, Dan Blake, Kevin and Diana Craig, Ginni Greer, Marty Grosjean, Leslie Hilleman, Gary Hoover, Mike Keegan, Meredith Lazaroff, the late Vern Lunsford, Randy Murphy, Gary Neben, Ken Nolan, Bob Reedy, Dan Stright, Charlie Winger, Gary Wolff, Jared Workman, and Laura Zaruba. Thanks to all of you for your patience while I documented routes and sometimes wandered off to check out variations to routes and approaches. Thanks also to CMC trip members who have accompanied me over the years on a number of these routes.

A special thanks to Kevin Craig for writing the chapter on equipment. Kevin, formerly the "Gear Guy" in *Trail and Timberline*, keeps abreast of developments in climbing equipment better than anyone else I know, and is always ready to share advice on the latest gear.

Many thanks to Gerry Roach for writing the Foreword. It was Gerry's books on the Indian Peaks Wilderness and Rocky Mountain National Park (the pocket-sized First Editions) that were the inspiration for many of our early snow climbs in those areas.

I would like to thank Kevin Craig, Ethan Greene and Dan Stright and many others for useful discussions on snow properties and avalanche awareness.

Excellent photos have been generously provided by Dan Bereck, Kevin Craig, Ginni Greer, Meredith Lazaroff, Randy Murphy, Dan Stright, Charlie Winger and Jared Workman.

Thanks to Kevin Craig, Ginni Greer, Meredith Lazaroff, Bob Reedy, Dan Stright, and Laura Zaruba, for reviewing drafts and offering suggestions to improve the text. I can't say enough about Ginni's hard work in proofreading the text at every level of production. Her diligence has been nothing short of heroic.

The final product is a result of the painstaking work by Alan Bernhard—design and composition, Dianne Nelson—copyeditor, and Alan Stark—publisher. Thanks for keeping me on the straight and narrow.

Special thanks to the people at National Geographic Maps for the use of their TOPO! Outdoor Recreation software for both mock-ups and final maps.

Long-time climbing mentors Charlie Winger and Dave Reeder deserve a special thanks. Their enthusiasm and attitude to climbing have had a profound impact on me.

FOREWORD

DAVE COOPER WAKES UP WITH HIS BOOTS ON. When most of us are just starting to crunch our morning granola, Dave is already crunching up a snow couloir with the snow flying in graceful arcs from his steady steps. Fueled by a passion for the heights, Dave has crafted creative routes across the spectrum of Colorado's highest peaks, and it's not surprising that he lives in the mountains. The rest of us are lucky that Dave also has a desire to share and that he crafts guidebooks like this one.

Colorado Snow Climbs is one of those books that has a place on the shelf before it is written. In spite of guides galore, Dave's tinctured tome fits perfectly between cumbersome compendiums. Dave cleverly organizes his forty-two climbs by season rather than by traditional geographic or rating divisions, and this really is a guide for all seasons. Better, the climbs are scattered across six of Colorado's ranges, and their difficulties offer challenges for every climber. I've done most of the climbs in this book and have also named many of them, so I can testify that the more of these climbs you do, the more you will appreciate this book.

I feel compelled to speak about the ever-changing medium of snow. Obviously, a snow route can change drastically by hour, day, month, year, and decade. Aspect, sun, and wind can reverse a fortune in minutes. With the climate turning flips between drought and flood, the best we can do is watch conditions carefully and make safe decisions. Earlier this year, I backed out of a couloir choked with rotten snow that was simply not intended to support a climber. I moved 200 yards around a corner and tackled another slope that was crampon hard. In a few minutes, my techniques went from swimming to front pointing, and the hazards varied from avalanche to a good old-fashioned fall.

In over a half century of mountaineering in Colorado, one of my scariest moments was on a snow climb—one that I am glad is not in this book. Poised high on the north face of North Maroon Peak, the snow softened faster than I could climb, and I found myself at the mercy of snow physics and the snow gods. With only ten feet to go to a ledge, I realized that the slope I was on was sagging toward a sure collapse and that my weight was the catalyst of my own destruction. It was not a time for strength moves. Delicately distributing my weight over a dozen areas, I eschewed the view of the valley between my legs and oozed up to the ledge.

Like an ascent, a snow route is transient, and on a thousand other occasions, I have reveled in snow's magnificent moods. Study Dave's descriptions carefully, but remember that the climbs that you do will be different than Dave's or mine, and that your success, safety, and joy will depend on your decisions. That is the way it should be.

GERRY ROACH
Boulder, Colorado
September 2007

PREFACE

THE CONCEPT FOR THIS BOOK EVOLVED OVER SEVERAL YEARS. Initially I simply wanted to put together a collection of favorite snow climbs that friends and I had enjoyed over the years. Then I realized that, more than any other factor (geographic location, for example), the season dictates when to climb a particular route. That is why the climbs in this book are arranged to follow the seasons. While it is impossible to predict exactly when a particular climb will be "in shape," given the climate variations from year to year, you may be able to calibrate a season by observing whether that season appears to be progressing more or less rapidly than the historical norm.

Catching a route "in shape" is uniquely satisfying, especially those climbs that may only exist for a matter of days. The search for the "perfect climb" is a never-ending pursuit. I hope that in this guide you will find some ideas for your "perfect climb."

Think of this guide as a sampler. There are endless possibilities for good snow climbs in Colorado. Perhaps after reading this book you will look at a mountain a little differently.

Early morning approach to the east face of Longs Peak.

INTRODUCTION

It has often been said that the mountains of Colorado provide some of the best training ground in the Continental United States for aspiring mountaineers.

Beyond the obvious advantages of being able to live and train at altitude, our mountains provide just about every type of terrain likely to be encountered in other ranges. The exception is that our glaciers are more like permanent snowfields; therefore, crevassed terrain is not often a concern.

Snow climbing is, for me, one of the most enjoyable mountaineering activities. It requires a wide variety of skills since, because of the ephemeral nature of the medium, conditions are constantly changing. A route that you expect to be a straightforward snow climb might, in a dry year or later in the season, become a mixed route requiring not only snow-climbing skills but also technical rock and ice skills.

I have attempted to indicate the wide variety of snow-climbing opportunities that exist almost year-round in Colorado's mountains. In the style of *Colorado Scrambles*, I've included some of the classic routes but also quite a few lesser-known but high-quality routes. You may notice the omission of many fine routes on Colorado's fourteeners. I feel that these have been well covered in great detail elsewhere, so apart from a couple of perennial favorites that I tend to climb every year, I've stayed away from them.

I hope there are climbs in this book that will appeal to climbers with a wide range of experience. The routes are primarily snow, but some of the climbs at the upper end of the difficulty range may require technical skills. No climbs in this guide would be classified as water ice climbs, but under certain conditions, some ice will be encountered. Difficult mixed routes are beyond the scope of this book, although under some conditions, a few of these routes might serve as a good introduction for the climber wishing to advance his or her skills.

The hardest pure rock climbing on any of these routes should be no more than 5.4 and not sustained, but with snow and ice on the holds and with either wet boots or with crampons on your feet, it is a good idea to protect with rock gear.

The changing climate conditions we are experiencing mean that the climbing season can vary from year to year. For that reason, you should monitor the snowpack and know its history. The best source for conditions information is the Colorado Avalanche Information Center (*http://avalanche.*

state.co.us/). I have attempted to give the best time of year for each climb, but this is only a rough estimate and varies from year to year.

Remember that the responsibility to assess conditions before starting a climb rests solely with you. Take an avalanche awareness course and regularly take refresher courses. Carry and know how to use avalanche safety equipment. Develop route-finding skills on snow. If you get up at 2 A.M. to do a climb, hike all the way in and then find conditions to be poor or dangerous, change your objective for the day and come back another time. None of us likes to be skunked on a climb, but it will still be there another time. Make sure you will be, too.

HOW THIS GUIDE IS ORGANIZED

Climbs in this guide are organized by season rather than by geography. This should allow the reader to select a suitable climb during any time of the year. I have attempted to include a wide range of climbs that cover the gamut from simple climbs, requiring little more than an ice ax, to technical routes demanding advanced climbing skills and much more technical equipment. Just because a route is included in one season doesn't always mean that it wouldn't be a fine climb in another season—it's just that conditions are likely to be more enjoyable in the season described.

I have a special affinity for the alpine ice that forms on Colorado's permanent snowfields during the autumn. This doesn't mean that the routes aren't good snow climbs during the summer. Some years, the alpine ice is covered by fresh snowfall before you will have a chance to climb it, putting the routes out of shape for that year. That again is the nature of snow climbing.

The seasonal snowpack begins to build in the fall as the storms become colder and as daytime temperatures begin to drop. The snow climate in Colorado's mountains is classified as continental, which means the storms produce low-density snow, the winters are cold, the winds are strong, and the seasonal snowpack is shallow (compared to coastal mountain ranges).

Starting with the winter season, this guide offers some of my favorite ridge routes. These ridges are where you are going to find the most consolidated snow and safest travel conditions. Expect everything from knife-edge snow ridges to sections of rock scrambling to short technical rock cruxes. Also included are one or two face and gully routes that, because of their location, tend to have better snow conditions for climbing.

Late winter and early spring is when the snow in south-facing couloirs becomes climbable, and typically the ridges are still in good shape. This is perhaps the prime season for snow climbs. Routes in this section range from straightforward, moderate snow climbs to those where the snow is not continuous and difficulties such as ice and rock may be encountered.

From late spring through summer, the snow on the ridges and south-facing slopes has melted out, and north-facing couloirs are the place to be. Also at this time of year, the permanent snowfields make good climbs, although as I mentioned, I prefer to catch them after the metamorphosis is complete and the snow is no longer white, but the gray of ice.

After new snow covers the alpine ice, usually sometime in October, conditions often never recover on those climbs, and you must look for other places to climb. November may be the only time of year when Colorado doesn't regularly offer good snow climbs. The ridges can still be climbed but usually have a few inches of slippery snow covering the rocks (not yet frozen in place), making the going a little tricky. And some years, the new snow is late in arriving and the alpine ice routes are still climbable.

EQUIPMENT CHAPTER

Kevin Craig has provided a comprehensive review of the equipment available to mountaineers, and discusses the advantages and disadvantages of the various components you might use to climb snow routes.

ROUTE DESCRIPTIONS

Each route description contains the following information:

ELEVATION GAIN. This is the accumulated round-trip elevation gain, including any elevation regained on the descent.

ROUND-TRIP DISTANCE. This is the distance in miles for the whole trip—car to car.

STARTING ELEVATION. This is the elevation at the parking area.

HIGHEST ELEVATION. This is usually the elevation at the top of the route.

BEST MONTHS TO CLIMB. This is the time of year when you are likely to find the conditions described, and probably the most difficult parameter to quantify.

DIFFICULTY. Technical difficulty and length are discussed here.

GEAR. This is what I would take on this climb. Depending on your comfort level and technical competence, you may elect to take more or less.

MAP. The USGS quad. Don't leave home without it!

Also included in each route description are driving directions, an introduction to the climb, comments and sometimes anecdotes from the climb, approach and descent information, and a description of the climb itself. Any known access issues are also discussed. I chose not to include a time estimate to complete a route. Snow conditions, both on the approach and on the climb, are so variable that time estimates are of little use. Expect long days on most of these routes and you won't be disappointed. I have climbed all of the routes described in this guide as day climbs, often starting in the dark. A number of the routes took up to fourteen hours to complete. If you have the time, you might consider breaking up the approach and plan your climb for two days for the longer routes.

Supplemental information for each route includes a map showing the route (and, sometimes, variations) and a list of GPS waypoints. This map is only meant to indicate the route location and does not replace a real USGS map for navigation.

A WORD ABOUT GPS DATA

Most of the routes shown on the maps were collected using a Magellan SporTrak Pro®. I've found it to perform better than many other models. A limitation seems to be that when you are climbing in a deep, narrow couloir (rather common with these routes), it sometimes loses the satellite signals for extended periods of time. I think that this is more likely an inherent limitation of the GPS system rather than a defect of the Magellan. I have tried to re-create these lost periods as accurately as I could. Similarly, a GPS waypoint collected under these conditions can be inaccurate. I hope that I've caught and fixed all of these anomalies, but remember that the route information provided is meant to be used *only as a guide*. You must choose a good route based on the conditions you find there that day.

All routes and waypoints were collected using the NAD83/WGS84 Datum.

RATINGS OF CLIMBS

Nowhere are ratings more subjective or variable than on snow climbs. The same route can go from being a moderate snow climb, to an alpine ice climb, to a mixed route, to a rock climb. You will often find different conditions than the ones described here. That's the nature of snow climbing. When I describe snow steepness, it usually refers to the average angle—that isn't going to change much. Local variations produced by wind and differential melting can change a climb quite a bit. I remember in particular a snow climb in the San Juans—it had a short section that was some of the steepest snow I'd climbed in Colorado. On other occasions, friends had found the same gully to be nothing more than a moderate snow climb.

Approach the difficulty ratings with an open mind.

SNOW STEEPNESS RATINGS

I see no way to improve on the system introduced by Gerry Roach. In this guide, snow steepness is defined as follows:

EASY: 0–30 degrees

MODERATE: 30–45 degrees

STEEP: 45–60 degrees

VERY STEEP: 60–80 degrees

VERTICAL: 80–90 degrees

ROCK RATINGS

Mountaineering: The Freedom of the Hills (6th edition, The Mountaineers) describes the following classes for rock climbing, based on the Yosemite Decimal System (YDS).

CLASS 2: Simple scrambling, with possible occasional use of the hands.

CLASS 3: Scrambling; a rope might be carried.

CLASS 4: Simple climbing, often with exposure. A rope is often used. A fall on Class 4 rock could be fatal. Typically, natural protection can easily be found.

CLASS 5: Where rock climbing begins in earnest. Climbing involves the use of a rope, belaying, and protection (natural or artificial) to protect the leader from a long fall. This class is subdivided into an open-ended decimal scale.

Rock sections of a route in this guide vary in difficulty between Class 2 and Class 5.4.

ALPINE ICE RATINGS

What is the difference between alpine ice (AI) and water ice (WI)? The answer is that it isn't always clear, but the definition used in this guide is as follows:

• Water ice is ice that forms when water flows then later freezes. Therefore, technically speaking, an ice section on Dreamweaver where meltwater has flowed over one of the rock steps and then refrozen should be given a WI rating.

• Alpine ice is the end point of snow metamorphism, when the snow has melted and refrozen (in place) countless times and has achieved a high degree of strength (sufficient to support substantial weight on the pick of an ice ax or tool).

It is generally accepted that AI and WI grades are roughly equivalent in difficulty. The alpine ice grades given to routes in this guide are as follows:

AI1: Flat ice.

AI2: Generally low-angled ice, where you need crampons and at least one ice tool or ax.

AI3: Steeper ice requiring crampons and two tools or one ax and one tool. The ice may not be well-attached.

AI4: Sustained technical climbing requiring crampons and two tools.

MIXED GRADES OF CLIMBING

A small number of routes in this guide have an "M" rating. These "mixed" climbs will require some rock climbing while you are wearing crampons and using either your hands or ice tools. The equivalence to rock-climbing grades is somewhat subjective, but a general consensus for the lower "M" grades might be as follows:

M1: Comparable to 5.5 rock climbing.

M2: Comparable to 5.6 rock climbing.

M3: Comparable to 5.7 rock climbing.

No route in this guide is rated harder than M3 under normal conditions.

SNOW FACTS FOR CLIMBERS

A book on snow climbing would not be complete without a discussion of the properties of snow and how these properties affect climbers. Not only should you consider the safety aspects relating to snow travel but also the properties of snow that create enjoyable and aesthetic climbing conditions. One of the main themes of this book is the changing nature of Colorado's snowpack through the seasons and how this metamorphism creates opportunities to climb snow routes on different types of terrain throughout the year. Another way of saying this is that there is a "natural" season for a snow climb of a given route.

A word about safety—there is no substitute for expert instruction. Take an avalanche awareness course and continue with refresher courses through the years. As you become more experienced, there is often a tendency to become somewhat casual about snow safety, and while some aspects of route selection and snow stability evaluation may become second nature, you always need to be conscious of your decision-making process. On one winter climbing trip, one of my partners asked why I hadn't taken a direct line to the summit. Initially not sure how to answer the question, I looked at our track and realized that what I had done was to stay clear of any convex slopes, where there tend to be higher stresses in the snowpack. I don't consider myself an expert in snow stability evaluation, but over the years I've taken enough classes and, equally important, have climbed and skied with experienced and careful friends, so that some of this knowledge has "rubbed off." The information reproduced here is not new, but I hope that reviewing it will be of value.

You cannot always remove all risk, but you can reduce that risk by becoming an intelligent user of the mountain environment.

Many of the snow safety texts focus on general mountain travel (skiing, snowshoeing, and snowmobiling), and while these are incredibly valuable, I feel that there are aspects of snow physics that relate specifically to climbers. In order to address some of these issues, the topic will be divided into three parts: Snow Physics, Avalanche Safety, and Route Finding.

Snow Physics

Snow climbs and avalanches both require snow. The seasonal snowpack is a layered structure, and each precipitation, wind, or sun event forms a new layer. There are thousands of ice crystals in each snow layer. The crystals are connected and form a coherent structure of ice and air spaces. Depending on how it forms, this structure can be quite weak or very strong. This is one reason why snow climbing is so enjoyable. In ideal conditions, it is easy to travel across this snow structure, and it is strong enough for climbing protection.

Water is one of the few materials on earth that naturally exists in all three phases: gas, liquid, and solid. The snow we climb in Colorado is very close to its triple point—the pressure and temperature where a material can exist in thermodynamic equilibrium. Near the triple point, materials are inherently unstable, as small changes in their environment can cause large changes in their strength. This is partly why a large snowstorm, rain event, or rapid temperature change can cause avalanches or make snow travel quite difficult.

Snow forms in clouds that are supersaturated with water vapor at below-freezing temperatures. Unlike ice, which forms from liquid water, snow crystals grow by condensation directly from the vapor phase through a process called sublimation. Snow crystal formation is a complex process that depends on temperature and humidity, among other factors.

Once it is on the ground, snow is transformed by compaction and metamorphism. These processes are mainly controlled by temperature and snow depth. However, other factors such as wind, solar radiation, vegetation, diurnal temperature fluctuations, liquid water content, and humidity also play a role. The snow pack consists of many layers resulting from multiple snowfalls, rain events, sun crust, surface hoar, wind-blown snow, and melt–refreeze ice layers. Ultimately, all of these layers, when buried by new snowfall or windblown snow, will experience metamorphism.

The water vapor pressure in the spaces between the snow crystals drives the changes that occur in the winter snowpack. The vapor pressure is largely determined by temperature, and this change in temperature through the snowpack is responsible for much of the metamorphism. Water mass sublimates from locally warm areas of the ice matrix and deposits on locally cold areas. The rate at which these changes occur and the characteristics of the resulting structure depend on the magnitude of the temperature changes in the snowpack, or the temperature gradient. A small temperature gradient causes less redistribution and hence slower crystal growth rates, while a higher temperature gradient leads to high growth rates. What is the result? Low growth rates create rounded crystals that tend to produce a well-bonded snow layer or a slab, while high growth rates are responsible for the creation of faceted snow, resulting in depth hoar (sometimes called sugar snow or TG snow) or surface hoar. Faceted snow creates weak layers that can fracture and produce avalanches.

Colorado is noted for its frequently weak snowpack. This is due to the climate of the Colorado mountains. The snow-covered ground is always near the freezing point of water. Snow depth and the air temperature determine the temperature gradient across the snowpack. During early winter in Colorado, we often have the worst-case scenario—shallow snow cover combined with cold air temperatures. The faceted snow, once formed, can persist all winter long, creating potentially unstable conditions.

One of the modifiers to the formation of TG snow is cloud cover, which changes the surface energy balance. A cloudy sky inhibits radiational cooling and tends to reduce the temperature gradient, while clear night skies result in strong radiational cooling and enhanced temperature gradient, often the cause of weak layer formation in midwinter. Conversely, in the springtime, cloud cover reduces refreezing of the snowpack at night, while clear skies help with a solid refreeze.

Wind also plays an important role in snowpack formation. Mechanical decomposition occurs when the ice crystals are broken apart, resulting in very small ice particles that pack together with small pore spaces between. This creates a very dense layer of snow called a hard slab and is also responsible for the creation of firm snow along ridges that provides good footing for climbers. The prevailing wind direction (usually from the west in Colorado) also determines where cornices form. These compacted snow features sometimes last well into summer and can create a significant objective hazard on many snow climbs.

The wind can also affect the heating and cooling of the snow. Mixing of the air just above the snow surface can slow the daily heating of the snow, in addition to contributing to a solid refreeze on a spring night.

Direct sun exposure can reduce the temperature gradient in the snow or heat it to its melting point. This causes the structure of the snow on sun-exposed slopes to be very different from that on shady slopes. Subtle changes in the aspect of the slope can produce large changes in the snow conditions. Icy layers, which can form a good sliding layer, may only exist on south-facing slopes, while the depth hoar may be most developed on north-facing slopes.

Avalanche Safety

The principal pieces of equipment that you should always carry in avalanche terrain are an avalanche transceiver, a shovel, and a probe pole. These are almost as important as your brain, a sophisticated and inexpensive device that can help you avoid the need to use these other devices. Other equipment that might be needed includes a first-aid kit, extra clothes and bivouac gear, plus items discussed in detail by Kevin in the equipment chapter. As Kevin mentions, the trade-off between carrying sufficient gear for an emergency and traveling light and fast is a complex issue.

Key to staying out of an avalanche is to understand what contributes to the hazard. Remember that the condition of any snow-climbing route cannot be reduced to simple equations or even rules-of-thumb. The only reasonable approach is to: (1) be aware of historical conditions; (2) read the avalanche forecast reports; (3) check the weather forecast; (4) leave early; (5) get to the route and assess the conditions; then (6) decide whether or not to climb.

Avalanche Hazards
In general, slab avalanches are much more dangerous than sluffs, though sluffs can kill you if they push you off of a climb or send you into a confined area such as a gully.

Remember that most people trigger the avalanche that kills them, and that the danger of triggering a dry avalanche increases and decreases over days and weeks, perhaps when we let our guard down.

In the spring, conditions change diurnally, and a natural release can occur due to cornice fall, water running along a bed surface, or localized heating of rock outcrops.

Ingredients of an Avalanche

For an avalanche to occur, there must be three ingredients present: a *slab* (something to slide), resting on a *weak layer* (something to break), resting on a *bed surface* (something to slide on). The bed surface can be a snow layer, the ground, or an artificial surface such as a roof.

Terrain Factors

Avalanche conditions are affected by both large- and small-scale terrain factors.

General Terrain Considerations

REGIONAL CHARACTERISTICS

Sometimes the location can be important. Conditions in the Wasatch Mountains of Utah are, in general, very different from those found in Colorado. Similarly, the San Juan mountains often exhibit a very different snowpack compared to, say, the Elks or Front Range mountains. You need to know the history of the snowpack for each range before you venture in.

ASPECT

The direction a slope faces has a large impact on the snowpack that forms there. In midwinter, north-facing slopes are exposed to the sun for very brief periods each day. The snowpack on these shady slopes tends to be much deeper with persistent weaknesses (depth hoar or TG snow). The sun shines on south-facing slopes for longer periods each day, producing hard, icy layers in the snowpack. These variations in snow conditions occur on both large and small scales. The north and south sides of a mountain can be as different as the sunny and shady side of a small ridge. On a climb of North Twilight in June, we were able to escape postholing in soft snow, to firm footing, just by moving a few degrees to the more northerly aspect. At the top of the route in the shade we found good cramponing snow.

WIND

Another dominant factor is the orientation of a slope relative to the wind. Wind will move snow from a windward slope onto a lee slope. Wind loading can occur across a major ridgeline but can also happen around any small terrain feature. Certain weather patterns will produce strong winds. You can

Wind can transport large amounts of snow in a short time span. We decided not climb our planned route the day this photo was taken. PHOTO BY DAVE COOPER

almost be assured that after the passage of a low-pressure system (storm-producing), the trailing high pressure will create a pressure gradient resulting in a wind event. Also, since our prevailing winter winds are from the west, north-south–trending ridges tend to be the ones to form cornices above the east faces.

ELEVATION

Another general rule is that the higher the elevation, the more snow falls due to orographic lifting in the atmosphere. Of course, this means more loading and hence more stress on the snowpack. The temperature also decreases with elevation in the lower atmosphere (troposphere). As previously discussed, colder air temperatures contribute to the formation of weak layers within the snowpack.

SLOPE ANGLE

Remember that releases are most likely to occur on slopes between 30 and 50 degrees. On steeper terrain, we tend to see spindrift avalanches that, while unpleasant to experience, usually have insufficient energy content to knock you off. This is because the energy is spread out over time rather than being stored and then released in a single event.

Localized Terrain Factors

TERRAIN TRAPS

These features increase the consequences of being caught in an avalanche. Areas to watch for include cliffs, where even a small avalanche can carry you over the edge, resulting in a big fall. Also watch for gullies, where a small avalanche can result in a deep burial, and obstacles such as rocks and trees, where a small avalanche can result in trauma (25 percent of the people killed in avalanches in the United States die from trauma and not from the burial).

Likely areas in which to trigger an avalanche: Convex slopes produce tension within the snowpack (similar to crevasses in glaciers). Rollovers are likely trigger points, because you have more tension and the slope angle is increasing. Concave slopes tend to give more support to the snowpack (from compression), but compression zones can also be dangerous when you have a collapsible, weak layer (surface hoar, depth hoar) in which a fracture can propagate from a low-angle zone into the start zone (steep area).

We know that thin spots tend to harbor weaker snow, but slope anchors, such as rocks and trees, are more complex in their contribution to overall slope stability. While these anchors disrupt the continuity of the slab and give support to the slab, they also produce localized areas of stress and snow weakness and therefore are common trigger points.

TYPE OF SLAB

A soft slab is defined as a slab that doesn't support your weight. This kind of slab is produced by snowfall and by light winds. Human-triggered soft slab avalanches tend to break near the area where the load is applied (i.e., at your feet).

A hard slab is defined as a slab with a hard, supporting surface that is formed by strong winds. In these slabs, cracks can propagate long distances. This allows you to walk out onto the slab before the avalanche releases—and this is *very, very* bad.

RAPIDLY CHANGING CONDITIONS

The snow can adjust to changes that occur slowly, but rapid changes produce catastrophic failure. Mechanisms that produce these rapid changes include increased loading caused by a snowstorm, wind loading, or your body weight.

Thermal effects can create problems—rapid warming causes or increases differential creep, creating stress in the snowpack, while rapid cooling makes material more brittle. The latter is a less common problem in Colorado, although I believe that this is often a major cause of instability in Canada. Rain on the snow is another cause, adding heat to the snow and eroding bonds.

The Human Factor

In fatal accidents, the victim, or a member of the victim's party, often triggers the avalanche. Common human-factor contributions include ignorance (not knowing there is a problem), overconfidence (not recognizing the severity of the problem), and distractions (everything from group dynamics to thinking about your job, relationships, etc.), which cause you to miss the obvious clues.

So what are some of the special issues that climbers face? We tend to be focused on the objective of the climb. The climb itself is often very steep and maybe too steep for avalanches. However, we often need to cross low-angle slopes to access the climb or to get down from the climb. These are common places for accidents. Climbers like to travel fast and light and often don't carry avalanche safety equipment.

We need to worry about the terrain above a climb, which often is not visible from below. The starting zone for an avalanche may be above the climb, and the avalanche may funnel into the route. In addition, low-angled benches on a route between steeper sections can accumulate deep snow.

Look for clues that may indicate signs of instability. Recent avalanches that have occurred on slopes of the same angle, aspect, and elevation as your planned route are a good indication that you should change your plans.

If cracks shoot out across the snow as you travel across a slope, get off the slope! The same is true if you hear "whumpfing" sounds, indicating a collapsing layer. Another indication of a potential problem is a hollow-sounding hard slab. This indicates a weak layer below. Remember that if you have to cross a suspect area, separate and cross one at a time, with the rest of the group observing each individual's progress.

Here are some questions to discuss among your group before venturing into potential avalanche terrain:

- Is the terrain capable of producing an avalanche?
- Can the snow slide? (Do we have all of the ingredients for an avalanche to occur?)
- Is the danger increasing (weather)?
- What will happen if one of us is caught in an avalanche on this slope?

Route Finding

To acquire proficiency in route finding takes years of experience. However, there are many things that you can do both before and during a trip that will increase your safety.

Planning

Make sure that you know and understand the route and identify landmarks on the map. Plan an approach and a descent route ahead of time, even if conditions in the field dictate a change (for example, it may be safer to rappel a route rather than exit onto loaded slopes above).

Be familiar with the snow history of the area. A good way to do this is to monitor snow conditions throughout the season by regularly checking conditions on the Colorado Avalanche Information Center website. This site is also a good place to check current conditions (know before you go). Understand the rated avalanche danger. You can often obtain information here that helps with the assessment of how well the new snow will bond to the old surface. An example of this might be when a storm comes in warm and creates an immediate bond to the old surface rather than falling on a cold, icy layer.

When you are looking at the weather forecast and planning your trip, look for events that will cause the avalanche danger to rise. These include large snowstorms or windstorms, as well as rapid temperature changes. Some examples are a frontal passage, downslope (chinook) winds, or clear and warm days directly after a snowstorm.

Know the wind direction in relation to your intended route. Also, consider whether recent precipitation (rain or snow) has occurred or will be occurring while you are out. Cloud-cover predictions can help you evaluate whether the spring snowpack will freeze solidly at night and whether wet slides will be likely during the daytime.

Managing Terrain

Ridges, low-angle slopes, and very high-angle slopes tend to be where travel is safest. Avoid rollovers and cornices. Identify and use islands of safety. Remember that rock outcroppings can provide solid protection if you're on a roped climb, but that they are also potential avalanche trigger points.

Don't cut a slope. It's better to go straight up than traverse across the slope. If you do have to cross a slope, cross well below the slope or at the top, not across the middle.

Lastly, understand what objective hazards you may be exposed to. This includes knowing what is above you and what is below. Remember that wind and sun can trigger avalanches way above you and that conditions above might be quite different from those at your location. Cornice collapse is a very serious problem, since the debris funnels down the gully or couloir, giving you no chance to escape. A note on cornices: I've seen them fall down not only when the sun hits them, but also when the temperature drops suddenly. Thus, any rapid change in temperature can be a problem.

The large and persistent cornice blocking the exit on Superstar (James Peak) illustrates one of the objective hazards confronting climbers on many snow climbs.   PHOTO BY DAVE COOPER

Of course, knowing what is below you is important because that is where you'll be taken by an avalanche or fall.

Being prudent, not paranoid, should allow you to enjoy a long and productive climbing career.

Dramatic views of The Flying Buttress from high on Dreamweaver.

PHOTO BY KEVIN CRAIG

EQUIPMENT

By Kevin Craig

It is virtually impossible to discuss mountaineering equipment, or "gear," without a concurrent discussion of style and risk. The history of mountaineering proves nothing if not that, given enough gear, any mountain can be beaten into submission. At the opposite end of the spectrum is "fast-'n-light," which requires, at *its* extremes, a fair dose of experience-and-good-judgment if practitioners don't want to end up good-and-dead.

To be sure, it is a pleasure to move through the alpine environment quickly and unencumbered. However, the fast and light climber or mountaineer must be aware of the reduced capability to deal with emergency situations and unexpected route conditions. You must come armed with the attitude and mindset that will enable you to turn around if conditions require more or different gear than expected, or, for example, if deteriorating weather would make an unexpected, unplanned-for night out potentially fatal rather than just uncomfortable. Even the world's most elite alpinists have come face-to-face in extremis with the question of how light is too light and the consequences of going "too light to go slow"—i.e., a lack of gear becoming a straightjacket that forces decisions and pace rather than being a liberating ethos. As will be discussed, sometimes skills and experience can replace some gear, but those skills must be well learned and carefully practiced in less-threatening circumstances before they become the difference between life and death.

All climbing and mountaineering involve balancing and the trading of risks. Some risks can only be avoided by staying home. These "objective" risks include rockfall, an unexpected winter storm, avalanches, and many others. These risks can be mitigated to a certain extent and in a variety of ways by skills and equipment:

ROCKFALL	Wearing a helmet Traveling only in the cold morning hours when rocks are still frozen to the mountain
STORMS	Checking the forecast Carrying a bivy sack Knowing how to construct snow shelters

AVALANCHE Careful snowpack evaluation and route selection
Carrying avalanche beacons, shovels, and probe poles

However, risks will always be present. And gear trades off with risk and skills in a variety of complex ways.

A key but often unexpressed aspect of the fast-and-light philosophy is that if conditions change or if you find conditions that you didn't plan for (verglas on a rocky section and you didn't bring crampons), you will have to turn around. Put simply, if you've brought a knife to a gunfight, admit it to yourself and come back another day when you're properly armed for the challenges.

It is virtually impossible in a guidebook such as this to provide detailed recommendations on every conceivable piece of clothing and equipment. Let's assume that you are familiar with the basic equipment required for hiking and mountaineering, at least in the summer season. Therefore, this discussion will only cover generalized aspects of the equipment required for snow climbs, as well as the particular applications of the "Ten Essential Systems" as they relate to climbs outside the summer season.

The recent broadening of the "Ten Essentials" to the "Ten Essential Systems" (as discussed in several recent instructional books) is particularly useful when you are planning gear for climbs in this guide, since they may be undertaken in all seasons.

To briefly reiterate, the essential systems are:
- Navigation
- Sun Protection
- Insulation
- Illumination
- First-aid supplies (and training)
- Fire
- Repair kit and tools
- Nutrition
- Hydration
- Emergency shelter

Add to these the specific tool systems required by the snow or technical climber who will be operating in a potentially remote or unfrequented environment:
- Flotation (skis, snowshoes, boots)
- Traction (ice ax, ice tool, type of boot, crampons, snowshoes)
- Protection (helmet, rock, ice, pickets)
- Rescue (avalanche gear, self-rescue classes, first aid)
- Communication (cell phones, radios, EPIRBS)

NAVIGATION

It's a long-held mountaineering tradition to never leave home without a map and compass. Indeed, no one should venture far from their vehicle or a maintained trail without decent real-world (i.e., a great deal more than book knowledge) map and compass skills. In good weather, and for the majority of peaks, few experienced climbers need more than a quick glance at the map and surrounding terrain to decide on a viable approach and ascent and descent routes. The key phrase in the previous sentence is "in good weather." Though perhaps not as common as in the Pacific Northwest or the Greater Ranges, whiteouts do happen in Colorado, especially in winter, and there's nothing quite like having a GPS in such conditions. A GPS also allows you to conveniently mark—and more importantly, reliably find—equipment stashes (e.g., snowshoes used on the approach) in any weather or terrain conditions.

Like any other piece of equipment, you should be very familiar with how to use a GPS before you rely on it, and you should carry backups—in this case, spare batteries and those aforementioned map and compass skills. Today, GPS units come in all sizes and shapes and have a fairly wide range of utility and performance. Above treeline, most any unit will probably provide good service, but if you expect to do many tricky approaches through dense forest or deep valleys, one of the units with a better antenna or advanced chip sets might be worth the money. All GPS units will allow you to upload routes or waypoints from popular PC mapping software (e.g., National Geographic's TOPO!®, Garmin's MapSource, etc.). Some will also allow you to upload topographic maps with varying levels of detail. The screen on many smaller units can be difficult to use for navigation in the field without a route uploaded at home. Regardless of the unit and software, be sure to practice in good weather and on familiar terrain before relying on the unit.

In good weather, a GPS can be simply a fun tool to track your progress and speed and tell you how far you are from the darned car at the end of a long day.

Without a GPS, you need to take much more careful note of landmarks on your approach and keep an even closer eye on the weather. If the clouds start to lower, begin planning on how you're going to find your way back, or turn around while you can still see *where* you're going. Don't overestimate how far you'll be able to see that distinctive rock formation if you end up in a true whiteout. Know where you are on the map, and know how to use "movable waypoints" with your compass (i.e., send your partner ahead on the correct bearing while you track him or her with your compass, have your friend stop and wait until you get to him or her, then repeat the process, leapfrogging in the correct heading).

Flagging (surveyors' tape) can also be used to mark critical route points. Just be sure to remove it on your descent.

SUN PROTECTION

Usually this is a combination of clothes and sunscreen. From late fall through (very) early spring in Colorado, sunscreen can be of a modest SPF. From the heart of spring onward, however, SPF 50 isn't a bad idea, nor is reapplying it several times throughout the day—a snow bowl at altitude makes a surprisingly and potentially painfully effective solar oven. Don't neglect your lips or the underside of your nose/nostrils—UV rays reflecting off of the snow can reach surprising places (including the inside of your mouth!).

INSULATION

The gold standard for warmth, low weight, and compressibility is goose down—the higher the "fill power" the better. The drawback of down, equally well known, is that when it gets wet, it loses virtually all of its insulating power. Synthetic insulation "fills" retain, to varying degrees, insulation power when they are wet, and some (Primaloft, Polarguard Delta, Exceloft) have made great strides in recent years in approaching the weight and insulating power of down. The primary issue, as of this writing, is that virtually no manufacturer produces a synthetic-fill jacket with a warmth rating that is anywhere close to the warmest down parkas. Most synthetic-fill parkas are "midweight" at best, and none approach the quantity of fill found in polar or 8,000-meter-peak-quality down parkas.

Nonetheless, if you are active or moving most of the day—and virtually all the climbs in this book are or can be completed in a day—synthetic-fill parkas are a very viable option. Synthetic fill is also a good idea if you may encounter rain or very wet snow or for multiday trips. If you know you'll be standing around more (e.g., belaying), will encounter mainly snow (especially dry Rockies snow), and will be back at the car by evening, down is hard to beat.

An important point if you are purchasing a synthetic-fill parka is to make sure that the shell material is breathable. If you're moving, you'll want that sweat to escape, and a breathable synthetic parka may allow you to dry out inner layers while on the move.

An important bit of "insulation" that's often overlooked is a hood on your jacket. It's amazing how much warmth this small bit of cloth adds to a jacket—largely due to how it puts a lid on the "chimney effect" (i.e., air warmed by your body core rising out through the neck of your hoodless jacket). Just make sure that when you buy a jacket, the hood will accommodate your helmet.

Don't forget adequate hand insulation either. I usually carry several pairs of gloves of varying warmth. Gloves with leather palms are important for durability if you expect to do much rope handling. Dexterity is important for all but the heaviest gloves—make sure that you can manipulate your gear (including pack buckles and other fasteners) with your gloves on.

Many companies make excellent gloves, so shop around and find a pair that matches your hand shape and finger length well.

ILLUMINATION

For many outdoor activities, the need for a headlamp means that something has gone wrong. Due to short winter days and the alpine starts required to catch firm spring snow, however, a good headlamp is an essential item in the snow climber's arsenal. Once the province of around-camp chores or tent-bound book reading, weight- and battery-saving LED headlamps have improved to the point where they are now very viable primary light sources for climbers and mountaineers.

Make sure that your headlamp attaches easily and securely to your helmet, and be sure to carry spare batteries and bulbs. Also, be sure that you can operate the controls while wearing bulky gloves. Lithium batteries (now available in AA and AAA sizes) have a much longer life in cold conditions, but at a significantly increased cost. Some climbers feel that rechargeable nickel metal hydride batteries (NiMH) provide a good compromise between life-cycle cost and cold endurance. Carrying spare batteries is also a good idea because few, if any, headlamps reliably indicate remaining battery power.

FIRST AID SUPPLIES

In this category, people vary a lot. Most guides seem to carry an ace bandage, some duct tape, a bandana, aspirin, and some Band-Aids. Other folks carry something close to a field surgery kit. For day trips, or even overnight climbs, though, the fact is that there's only so much that can be done in the field unless you're a trauma surgeon or combat medic. Generally speaking, you should have something to stop excessive bleeding and to support or immobilize an injured joint. Carry medications for pain and something for scrapes and cuts. Anything outside of that and you can either walk out or you'll be calling for rescue. A better investment of time and money is to get training in wilderness first aid, preferably a wilderness first responder (WFR) class that will teach you when self-rescue or self-evacuation is possible, how to stabilize a patient until help arrives (for really serious injuries), how to improvise with what you have on hand, and how to tell how scared you should (or should not) be.

FIRE

Because most snow climbs occur above treeline and many take place in the winter, "fire" in this context means a stove or the certain ability to get back near treeline, plus a lighter and fire-starter/tinder. In late spring through early fall, the latter option may be the best, and you generally will have other options for obtaining water (besides melting snow), and the warmth provided by a fire will be somewhat less critical. In winter, however, when days are short, the weather is uncertain and more of a threat, and injuries can be more life-threatening, a stove should be seriously considered if you venture anywhere beyond the reach of ready assistance. There are many compact, lightweight stoves on the market today. Be aware, though, that in cold temperatures canister fuel can be problematic, and regardless of stove type, you will probably have to build some kind of windbreak for your stove (perhaps a pit in the snow). All that said, carrying some fire-starting materials year-round for emergencies is a good idea. There are many commercial and some homemade fire starters: Trioxane (dirt cheap at the army surplus store), Esbit tabs, wax melted over dryer lint or wood shavings in a cellulose egg carton, etc. Whatever your preferred method, make sure that you have it down pat before venturing out and potentially betting your (or your partner's) life on it.

REPAIR KIT AND TOOLS

Sooner or later, all gear breaks. The impact can be anything from inconvenient to a life-threatening situation. Unfortunately, it's also not practical to carry spares of everything that might break or the tools/parts to repair any possible failure. By far the best way to deal with repairs is to avoid them in the first place. Take good care of your gear and give it a good inspection after every trip. Deal with small issues/repairs before they become big ones. A small multitool, some wire, plus the ever-present duct tape will address many issues sufficiently to get you back to the car. For longer routes or ones requiring more specialized gear (ice tools, crampons), consider carrying at least one spare of critical bolts, picks, etc. If you and your partner use the same make and model of gear, you can save weight by carrying one spare for the two of you. Don't hesitate to turn back if a critical piece of gear breaks or malfunctions. Also, be careful not to underestimate the impact of a gear failure; most mountaineering accidents are the result of an accumulated series of small errors or problems. A broken snowshoe may cause you to choose a more difficult snow-free ridge route, for example.

NUTRITION AND HYDRATION

An average climber with a modest winter snow-climbing pack hiking at altitude in moderately cold temperatures can burn more than 5,000 calories per day! Replacing that energy is important not only for completing the climb but also for staying warm and keeping your brain well fed so that you make good decisions. Difficult as it is during an alpine start, make sure to eat as good a breakfast as possible. Especially in winter, start the day with a healthy dose of long-burning fat to stay warm and energized throughout the climb. Eat something at regular intervals (at least once per hour) rather than on a "city" schedule. Keep snacks handy in your jacket or pants pockets for easy recharging. There are numerous good and convenient energy foods on the market today, including bars, gels, blocks, and liquids. Many companies make good energy drinks with various other claimed benefits as well. Note that a dilute (6 to 8 percent) carbohydrate solution is absorbed as well or better by the body than plain water. In addition, it provides extra energy. Not *all* the marketing claims are empty hype. It's also important to drink in order to metabolize those concentrated foodstuffs. The highest-tech sports gel won't do you much good if your body doesn't have enough fluid to metabolize it efficiently.

Above all, stay hydrated. Once you are dehydrated, your performance can suffer for days afterward! As little as 2 percent of your body weight lost in water (sweat) can begin to affect athletic performance. Some people can lose 2 to 3 liters of water per hour due to sweating during heavy exercise in a warm climate. Even at moderate temperatures, sweat loss can exceed 1 liter per hour. In winter, you also lose water by breathing—when you can "see your breath" when you exhale, that's your body's water condensing in the cold air.

So it's important to drink enough water, but do you have to carry all that water and associated weight?

Many climbers carry as little water as possible on a route if there are ample opportunities to replenish their supply (streams, snowmelt, springs, etc.) If this is your strategy, the extra weight of a water filter or chemical treatment is more than made up by the weight savings in water carried (a pint is a pound, after all!). In the winter, the trade-off is somewhat less obvious, since replenishing on-route means carrying a stove and fuel and taking a much longer break to melt snow. In Colorado winters, carrying enough water is usually the better solution, because most climbs aren't long enough to justify the effort and time of "brewing up" by melting snow along the way.

When the temperature stays above freezing, a hydration system (e.g., Camelbak™) can be a convenient way to stay hydrated. The main drawback is that it can be hard to monitor your fluid consumption in order to "stretch" your water throughout the length of a climb. In the long run, though, it may be better to replenish your water along the way and drink up!

Below about 25°F, hydration systems are generally more trouble than they're worth. If you decide to use a hydration system anyway, start the day with warm liquid, get some insulation for the hose, stash it inside your jacket, and ALWAYS blow the liquid back into the reservoir after taking a drink. Also, carry an empty, spare bottle for when your hydration system freezes up despite all your precautions.

If you use bottles in winter, you'll want water bottle "parkas" to keep them from freezing to whatever extent possible. It's a good idea to start the day with boiling water (or a sports drink) in the bottles as well. A good tip is to wrap your spare bottle(s) inside your next layer inside your pack. The heat lost from the bottle will warm up your jacket—there's nothing like putting on a nice cozy warm jacket when you need that next layer. If it's extremely cold and/or your bottles are starting to freeze up, stash them in the parka upside down—ice forms from the top down and you don't want the neck of the bottle freezing solid. Large-mouthed bottles seem to be less prone to freezing up.

EMERGENCY SHELTER

This is another area where options and equipment can vary enormously with season and with your experience and expertise.

Though few if any climbs in this book require carrying a tent, a prudent climber will always consider emergency shelter that may be required if one becomes injured, gets lost on the approach or descent, or gets pinned down by weather. Even a decision *not* to carry shelter carries with it added risk and the requirement that the climber watch the weather more carefully and be more willing to turn around if conditions deteriorate.

Emergency shelter can be as simple as a heavy tarp or space blanket in the summer or a shovel in the winter (if the snow is deep enough and you know how to construct snow shelters). A lightweight bivy sack and extra insulating layers may also be adequate in all but the most severe conditions. Some alpine climbing packs have a snow skirt to provide an "elephant-foot" bivy sack, while many also contain a foam pad that can be removed and used in a bivy situation.

Again, the key aspect is to carefully consider the trade-offs between weight, speed, and safety and to be absolutely familiar with whatever system you are relying on. Test out your system in low-risk situations—e.g., "bivy" next to the car on a nasty winter night. Go out for a fun day of snow-shelter building (and testing) at a nearby mountain pass on a bluebird winter or spring day.

TRACTION AND FLOTATION

For some snow climbs, all that is required is a good pair of boots. Boots used for snow climbing need to be sturdy in order to serve as a solid platform for crampon attachment, protect your feet, and enable you to kick reliable steps in firm snow. The side of the soles and the back of the heel should have a solid and square profile (rather than a rounded profile) in order to "cut" steps when you are traversing firm snow slopes and to provide traction when you are plunge-stepping down moderate to soft snow.

For approaches and descents, especially in winter and spring, a pair of snowshoes is often a requirement that will save hours of unpleasant wallowing. Snowshoe design has undergone several revolutions in recent years. Make sure to get a well-built pair that will provide good traction when you are traversing slopes (or "side-hilling") as well as when you are going straight up and down. Some models feature a wire bail that can be raised under the heel to ease calf strain on steep ascents. Models that feature a binding system that's easy to use while wearing gloves or mittens are a real plus when it's cold and the wind is howling. Also make sure that the snowshoes can be attached to your pack for those days when the snowpack stays firm all day or when it is unexpectedly melted on your approach. Be sure to know how the binding system attaches to the boot, and give some thought as to how you might make a field repair. Being stuck several miles "in" with deep snow and a broken snowshoe is no fun.

Some climbers use skis for ascent and (more fun) descent of snow routes. For most skiers, this is normally practical only from perhaps midwinter through mid to late spring. The use of skis for mountain travel (ski mountaineering) requires considerable skill and experience and is outside the scope of this guidebook. Refer to any of the excellent ski mountaineering guides, and get expert instruction.

To travel safely over (and up!) well-frozen spring snowpack, fully transformed summer snow, and fall alpine ice, crampons are a necessity. Many companies currently make high-quality crampons that attach in a variety of ways. The classic step-in binding is the lightest and works well if your boots have the requisite toe and heel welts for the toe bail and heel lever. Many spring/summer boots have only a heel shelf for a heel lever and require a hybrid crampon binding consisting of a plastic cage in the front and a heel lever in the back (so-called "New-matic"™ bindings). These also work very well, even on terrain that is quite technical. Crampons are also available that have a plastic cage in the front and rear and work with virtually any boot (or even approach shoes). Generally speaking, these (and the associated soft boots) are suitable only for the lowest angled routes and probably will not provide the desired stability on very firm snow or ice.

Traditionally, crampons have been made of steel, but several manufacturers now produce quality aluminum crampons that will save about 50 percent of the weight of steel crampons. These are mostly available with hybrid or full-cage bindings and work well if you expect only to encounter nothing harder than firm snow and won't need to travel extensively over rocky sections between the snow portions of the climb. Aluminum is much less durable than steel, dulls quickly on rock, and is not easy to resharpen effectively.

In terms of crampon style, twelve point steel crampons with horizontal front points are the most durable and versatile. The horizontal front points are less likely to shear through snow that is less firm, and perform quite well on ice up to and including vertical waterfall ice (if you should someday decide to try ice climbing). Ten point crampons normally lack a set of secondary points behind the front-points, which provide welcome support and added traction when "front-pointing" on steeper slopes. Avoid specialized ice climbing crampons, especially those with vertical, "cookie cutter" rails. These are uncomfortable for walking on less steep terrain and are more prone to accumulating snowballs underfoot, which can dangerously reduce traction. Whatever crampons you decide on, you should purchase or make your own "anti-balling" plates since even the most flexible glacier-walking crampons can be subject to snow-balling under certain conditions.

A boot that is at least semi-rigid, and crampons with a step-in or hybrid binding, will make your life much easier on routes in this book—like Dreamweaver, Flying Dutchman, or Martha, which have sections of very steep snow and ice. For winter climbing, an insulated boot is also worth considering. This can either be a classic plastic double boot or one of the many excellent insulated single boots on the market today. For overnight climbs in winter, however, you will want a double boot so that you can keep the liner in your sleeping bag to dry out and stay warm.

For many of the climbs in this book, a single mountaineering-style ice ax is adequate. The length of a mountaineering ax is very much a matter of personal preference, but in general, the steeper the route, the shorter the ax you'll want. On snow less than about 40 degrees, a "standard-length" ax works for most people. This is one on which the spike reaches ankle level when held at arm's length by your side while holding the head. Steeper than 40 degrees and you'll want a shorter ax, and once you approach climbs of 50 to 60 degrees, you may want something as short as an ice tool (i.e., approximately 55 centimeters) plus a second tool. Although modern axes are increasingly light in weight, the overall design has not changed much. In the last couple of years, some mountaineering axes have incorporated a mild curve in the upper shaft that adds some clearance when the ax is swung overhead. Surprisingly, this curve does not compromise the use of these axes for self-belay or self-arrest, so there's not a lot of downside if one of these has caught your eye. Don't go too far down the lightweight path for an ax, however—some of the very lightest have aluminum heads that do not work well for anything but soft snow. You'll be very disappointed if you try to use one of these on alpine or water ice even if only for a move or two.

For the steepest routes in this book, and for any that have water ice or alpine ice, a second ax will add comfort and efficiency. Most climbers use an ice tool for this purpose. Straight shaft ice tools work very well for plunging by the shaft but are almost impossible to find these days. Fortunately, almost any ice tool with a sturdy, sharp spike and without too much of a "pinkie rest" on it will work well as a second tool. Avoid the radical tools now available for modern mixed climbing ("M" climbing); they are special-purpose tools, and the purpose is not snow climbing.

It goes without saying that you should be exquisitely familiar with all of the techniques associated with using an ice ax and crampons before you set out to use them on one of these climbs. Self-belay, self-arrest (from all positions with a pack on), piolet traction, piolet ancre, French (pied platte, en canard, etc.), and German and American techniques should all be second nature to you before you attempt these climbs. Steep, frozen snow gullies are the place to employ these techniques, not to learn them.

PROTECTION

The one item that should absolutely go with you on any snow climb (besides an ax and boots) is a helmet. The author experienced at least some rockfall on virtually every route in this book—including one near-death experience. Make sure that your helmet fits well over any potential layers you may wear on your head and that it has some way of securing a headlamp. It doesn't matter much whether your helmet is of the foam or hardshell type as long as it is approved by the UIAA for mountaineering use and you wear it!

Due to the frequent lack of a deep, firm snowpack in Colorado, pickets may be of limited use. Most often, to be completely secure, they need to be buried "T-slot" fashion, which can be time-prohibitive. To be reliable in a "normal" vertical placement, a picket should have to be hammered into the snow. Frequently, the best protection can be had using rock gear in the side of a couloir. It goes without saying that you should get expert instruction in placing and evaluating rock protection before you rely on it. Another important point is that you should never rope up without placing some kind of protection, whether on lead or while simul-climbing. Countless climbers have been injured or killed by violating this simple rule or by overestimating the ability of one person's self-arrest skills to protect an entire rope team. Don't do it.

Ice screws can often provide reliable protection in winter, on shady spring climbs, or on hard, fall alpine ice. Again, obtain competent instruction in the use and evaluation of ice protection before you bet your life on it.

A rope and harness connect your body to the rock, snow or ice protection that you've placed. Although it is always safest to use a rope that is rated as a "single rope," most snow climbs occur on terrain that is considerably less than vertical so potential fall forces are also considerably less than those imagined when the strength test for single ropes was designed. The likelihood of the ropes being stressed across a sharp edge is similarly low on a snow climb, as compared to a rock climb, so the need for a thicker (9.5 millimeter to 10.5 millimeter) single rope is similarly less. For these reasons, many snow climbers, when they feel the need for protection, will use one rope from a pair of "half" (sometimes called "double") ropes. These are normally 8 millimeter to 9 millimeter in diameter and are indicated by the fraction inside a circle on the label at the ends of the rope. The weight difference between a 10.5 millimeter single rope and one 8.1 millimeter half-rope can be over 2 pounds (for a 60 meter length)! Often a 50 meter (or even shorter) length of rope is more than sufficient for most snow climbs as well—a further weight savings.

Many manufacturers make quality lightweight harnesses. If you want to use a harness year-round, adjustable leg loops are a necessity. This allows adjustment for differing thickness and layers of clothing between summer and winter. Leg loops that can be completely undone so that the harness can be put on and removed without stepping through the leg loops may be convenient if you ever find yourself needing to don a harness on a narrow ledge or steep snow slope. The degree of padding is a matter of personal choice and comfort. In winter, your heavier clothing often provides adequate padding. In any case, you are much less likely to spend a considerable amount of time hanging in a harness while snow climbing, so the level of padding may depend on whether you want one harness for all of your climbing activities or intend to acquire two or more for different types of climbing (snow, rock, ice, alpine, etc.). Unless your pack has gear loops on the waist-belt you will want to have gear loops on your harness (some of the very lightest alpine harnesses come without these).

RESCUE

Avalanche gear tends to be a matter of taste among snow (and ice) climbers. The general feeling is that couloirs and ice gullies are such ideal terrain traps, and the terrain is so steep, that one's chances of survival during the initial slide are not high enough to warrant the added weight of avalanche rescue gear. If conditions are that bad, the thinking goes, you shouldn't be doing the climb in the first place. Nonetheless, conditions at the top of a climb aren't always the same as they are at the bottom, and the sun changes everything. Carrying avalanche rescue gear unarguably stacks the odds in your favor, even if only by a bit. In any case, all climbers and mountaineers should strive to become experts in avalanche prediction and hazard evaluation. Take as many classes as you can, read the professional forecasts, and practice, practice, practice with your avalanche beacon.

In addition to some sort of advanced first-aid training, if you are engaged in any kind of technical climbing in the backcountry, invest in a technical self-rescue class. This will give you the basic tools necessary to get your partner to a relatively safe location where you can stabilize him or her, after which you can either walk out or summon help, as appropriate. As with technical climbing skills, however, you need to practice rescue skills on a regular basis.

COMMUNICATION

Communication in the backcountry generates some heated opinions. Many people are deeply offended if someone makes a cell phone call from the summit of a peak. While coverage is far from universal, it's also undeniable that cell phone use has saved more than one life or limb when bad things have happened—as they sometimes do. Follow your own ethos on this one, but also recognize that you may be foregoing an important lifeline.

Family Radio Service (FRS) radios are becoming increasingly popular for technical climbing. While most regular partners develop their own communication system (often conveyed solely by rope movement), when things don't go as planned and the wind is howling or ripping your shouts from your throat, radios allow detailed and nuanced communication. Again, weigh the risks and benefits and make a reasoned decision.

Within the last couple of years, personal emergency satellite beacons have become readily available if not readily affordable. While they almost guarantee some kind of response, it is a one-way communication—there is no way to tell rescuers exactly what help you need. They are yet another lifeline worth considering, especially for remote trips, but should not be a substitute for having competent partners and for leaving a detailed itinerary and expected return time with friends or family.

PACK

Lastly, you will need some sort of pack to contain all of this gear. Pack design and materials of construction have made great strides in recent years. It is now common for 40 to 50 liter packs that can "comfortably" carry loads in excess of 40 pounds to weigh-in at less than three pounds! While we should all strive to minimize weight as much as we safely can, a snow climb may require snowshoes for the approach, helmet, ice ax and crampons plus a rope, harness and protection for the climb, and you may want to have a stove and/or bivy sack along in the winter. This gear adds up very quickly to a significant load, so make sure to load up a prospective pack in the store before you buy it and make sure it will comfortably carry the weight. You'll also want to be sure the pack has places to attach all of this gear, since for some climbs, you'll need to carry all of it at the same time. Also be sure that the top lid of the pack does not interfere with tilting your head back to look up the mountain when that pack is loaded and you have your helmet on— more than one climber has experienced this problem with a pack that otherwise works well for them.

Items Needed for All Climbs
- Ice ax
- Helmet
- Sturdy boots
- Ten essential systems
- Good judgment
- Good attitude
- Good friends

Specialty Items to Consider by Season(s)

WINTER/SPRING
- Balaclava and goggles
- Stove
- "Enhanced" shelter (e.g., bivy sack)
- Avalanche gear
- Snowshoes or skis
- Bottle parkas
- Heavy (i.e., very warm) down or synthetic parka
- Heavy gloves/mittens

SPRING/SUMMER
- Water filter or chemical treatment
- Hydration system
- "Glacier" hat

SUMMER/FALL
- Ice screws
- Sharp crampons

PHOTO BY DAVE COOPER

Looking down the west ridge of "Atlantic Peak." This ridge offers a good introduction to winter ridge climbing.

PHOTO BY DAVE COOPER

1. "Atlantic Peak"—West Ridge

ELEVATION GAIN	2,900 feet
ROUND-TRIP DISTANCE	5.4 miles
STARTING ELEVATION	10,991 feet
HIGHEST ELEVATION	13,841 feet
BEST MONTHS TO CLIMB	December through April
DIFFICULTY	A moderate winter mountaineering outing on an exposed ridge
GEAR	Snowshoes and ice ax (crampons optional, depending on conditions)
MAP	Copper Mountain 7.5 minute

GETTING THERE: Take exit 195 off Interstate 70 and follow the signs for Colorado 91 to Leadville. (This is also the exit for Copper Mountain.) Drive south on Colorado 91 for 6.4 miles and park in a large plowed parking area on the east side of the highway, 5.3 miles north of Fremont Pass.

COMMENT: Winter mountaineering provides the opportunity to experience Colorado at its most spectacular. It also gives the aspiring mountaineer additional challenges that can turn an easy "walk-up" route in the summer into an exciting and rewarding outing. The west ridge of "Atlantic Peak" is such a case. (Note: "Atlantic Peak" is not an officially named peak, hence the quotation marks. On the map it is shown as Peak 13,841.) Conditions in the summer categorize the ridge as Class 2, but the knife edge formed by winter snow makes this route a fine introduction to more exposed snow climbing. Friends and I have long used this outing for expedition training.

Snowshoes are best for this trip. I have tried it with skis in the past, and while they are great on the approach, the lower part of the ridge often has lots of exposed rocks that are challenging during a downhill ski run. While we haven't needed to use crampons on this ridge, sometimes the snow can be hard enough that they would have been useful in a couple of spots.

APPROACH: From the parking area, snowshoe up the four-wheel-drive road for 1.1 miles to a point directly opposite Pacific Creek. Leave the road here and cross Mayflower Gulch, then start to climb up through the trees, heading for the saddle between "Atlantic" and Mayflower Hill. As you reach treeline, carefully choose a route up the broad start to "Atlantic's" west ridge. Usually this ridge is wind-scoured with lots of exposed rocks, but after a

The ridge alternates between moderate snow climbing and talus.   PHOTO BY DAVE COOPER

heavy snowfall it may have some avalanche potential. Take care and know the snow conditions.

THE CLIMB: After gaining 400 feet, the ridge flattens out for a while before narrowing and steepening again. This is a good spot to take off the snowshoes and take out the ice ax. The approach is over! Climb up mixed snow and talus from this point to the summit. The ridge seems to go on forever, especially when wind is combined with subzero temperatures, as it often is at this time of year. The climbing is never difficult, but the mixture of rock and snow can be tricky. While cornices rarely form on the ridge, it is quite common to find a moderate knife-edge section of the ridge that can provide some excitement. Be careful to avoid unstable snow slopes—the ridge-top is usually the best place to be. When you reach the top, the views are excellent. Mayflower Gulch offers some of the most rugged terrain in the area.

DESCENT: Head back down the ridge.

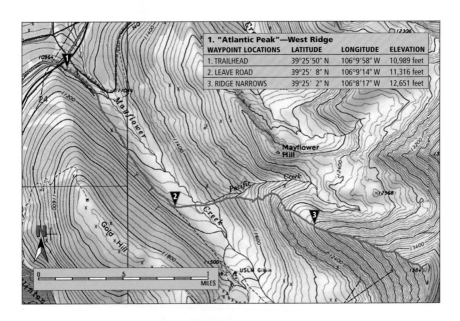

1. "Atlantic Peak"—West Ridge			
WAYPOINT LOCATIONS	LATITUDE	LONGITUDE	ELEVATION
1. TRAILHEAD	39°25′50″ N	106°9′58″ W	10,989 feet
2. LEAVE ROAD	39°25′ 8″ N	106°9′14″ W	11,316 feet
3. RIDGE NARROWS	39°25′ 2″ N	106°8′17″ W	12,651 feet

The wind creates
dramatic snow
sculptures.

The long west ridge of "Drift Peak" is a starkly beautiful and remote place in the winter.

2. Fletcher Mountain via "Drift Peak"

ELEVATION GAIN	2,900 feet
ROUND-TRIP DISTANCE	5.4 miles
STARTING ELEVATION	10,991 feet
HIGHEST ELEVATION	13,951 feet
BEST MONTHS TO CLIMB	December through May, with April and May being best for the extended outing
DIFFICULTY	A strenuous winter mountaineering outing on an exposed ridge to the summit of "Drift Peak;" moderate ridge running plus one short technical section (lower Class 5), which will require a 30-foot rappel on the return
GEAR	Snowshoes and ice ax (crampons optional, depending on conditions); if you continue to the summit of Fletcher, you'll need a rope and rock protection; don't forget to take your headlamp
MAP	Copper Mountain 7.5 minute

GETTING THERE: Take exit 195 off Interstate 70 and follow the signs for Colorado 91 to Leadville. (This is also the exit for Copper Mountain.) Drive south on Colorado 91 for 6.4 miles and park in a large plowed parking area on the east side of the highway. This is 5.3 miles north of Fremont Pass.

COMMENT: The west ridge of "Drift Peak" offers a fine winter or spring outing. The climbing is varied and, while not technical, will often keep your attention. Continue over to Fletcher on the challenging connecting ridge and add a short technical mixed crux. Even if you stop at the summit of "Drift Peak," you will find plenty of scrambling on rock and snow. Expect a full day, depending on the snow conditions you encounter. Adding Fletcher makes for a very long day.

"Drift Peak" is the unofficial name of Unnamed 13,900, a subpeak of Fletcher Mountain. Its east ridge forms the right-hand skyline of rugged Mayflower Gulch.

This ridge has been the scene of a number of accidents. Friends and I had a close call on one occasion when a spring "thunder-snow" event caused us to turn around and hurry down the ridge. With metal parts buzzing and whiteout conditions, we attempted to descend the ridge too quickly. I stepped off the ridge at one point and would have gone all the way down if not for a desperate plunge of my ice ax into the ridge as I fell. After getting back onto the ridge, we started down again, only to have almost the same

thing happen to one of my climbing partners, again with no serious consequences. After that we took things a little more cautiously.

APPROACH: From the parking area, snowshoe or ski up the four-wheel-drive road for 1.5 miles to a point where the trail divides just before the cabins of the old Boston Mine.

THE CLIMB: Start climbing southwest up to the ridge, using terrain features to avoid avalanche potential, including the cornices that form regularly. Once you are on the ridge, head up toward the first steep section at 12,200 feet, a good place to take off skis or snowshoes. From here, the route should be obvious. If the talus is frozen, the climbing can be very pleasant; if not, the loose slopes can be somewhat tedious.

Once you are up the first steep section, the gradient eases for a while. Usually this part offers nice snow climbing with an occasional Class 3 rock step. The ridge is quite narrow in spots and requires some care, especially in bad weather conditions. At about 12,700 feet, the ridge again steepens and also becomes slightly more complex, requiring a bit of route finding. Generally, the ridge crest is the best place to be to avoid avalanche hazards.

Climbing the rock step between "Drift" and Fletcher.

PHOTO BY DAVE COOPER

After what seems a long time, you will finally reach the summit of "Drift." Now the fun begins. Before committing to the traverse to Fletcher, evaluate the group's strength, the time of day, and the weather conditions. It may be necessary to wait for the longer days of spring before attempting this extension to the climb. If you decide to continue, descend the northeast ridge of "Drift" to a notch—the technical crux of the route. Carefully down climb into the notch, possibly using a ramp on the left (northwest) side of the ridge. Once you are in the notch, a short, lower Class 5 climb is necessary to gain the far side. In summer this is often soloed, but with snow over rock and wet boots it is advisable to use a rope and place a couple of pieces of protection.

Once you are past the notch, the difficulties are over, but the work is not. Descend on snow to the "Drift"/Fletcher saddle, then climb up Fletcher's southwest ridge, again on snow.

DESCENT: To descend, retrace your steps, rappelling into the notch and then continuing back over to "Drift" and down the west ridge. Depending on snow conditions, this may appear to take almost as long as the ascent.

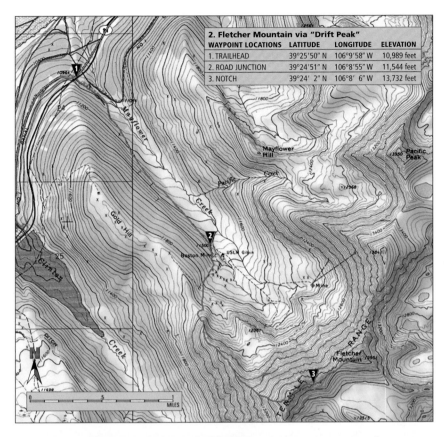

2. Fletcher Mountain via "Drift Peak"			
WAYPOINT LOCATIONS	LATITUDE	LONGITUDE	ELEVATION
1. TRAILHEAD	39°25'50" N	106°9'58" W	10,989 feet
2. ROAD JUNCTION	39°24'51" N	106°8'55" W	11,544 feet
3. NOTCH	39°24' 2" N	106°8' 6" W	13,732 feet

The east ridge of "Drift Peak", seen from Mayflower Gulch. The ridge climb begins to the right of the rightmost ridge point shown here.

PHOTO BY DAVE COOPER

Climbers heading over one of the many minor ridge points on their descent from Grizzly Peak, reminding us that we are only halfway when we reach the summit. PHOTO BY DAVE COOPER

3. Grizzly Peak

ELEVATION GAIN	2,900 feet of total elevation gain (750 feet of this is climbed on the descent)
ROUND-TRIP DISTANCE	5.6 miles
STARTING ELEVATION	10,814 feet
HIGHEST ELEVATION	13,427 feet
BEST MONTHS TO CLIMB	December through May
DIFFICULTY	Easy snow climbing on a high ridge
GEAR	Ice ax
MAP	Grays Peak 7.5 minute

GETTING THERE: Drive to Loveland Pass on U.S. 6.

COMMENT: On a day when avalanche danger makes it unwise to venture onto most of the peaks in the area, consider a climb of Grizzly Peak. Or, head up here if you just want to enjoy a high-altitude romp above treeline with outstanding views. The ridges tend to alternate between sections that are blown clear of snow and sections of good, hard, wind-packed snow. Therefore, you can probably leave the snowshoes at home on this one. The main dangers to watch out for are large cornices that regularly form along the ridge, plus high winds and whiteout conditions that can make route finding difficult. Of course, it is still important to exercise caution in any areas that could potentially slide, but avalanche potential on this route is generally low to moderate.

On a good spring day, you can extend the trip to include the traverse over to Torreys Peak and Grays Peak, then descend Stevens Gulch. If you're willing to carry skis all the way, the descent from the summit of Grays offers some great spring skiing. Obviously, the logistics for this extension are a little more complicated, because you need to set up a car shuttle between trailheads. The statistics quoted do not include this extension.

APPROACH: None.

THE CLIMB: From the parking area at the top of the pass, head northeast up the broad, gentle ridge to the point where this ridge intersects the main north ridge of Grizzly Peak at 12,915 feet. It is important to note this point where the ridges connect, because it can be a little confusing on the descent if visibility is low. You may want to leave some flagging (surveyors' tape,

Climbers approaching the final summit ridge of Grizzly Peak.   PHOTO BY DAVE COOPER

which you should remove on your way down) or use a GPS to record the location. Turn right (southeast), and follow the ridge with its multitude of ridge points, all of which need to be negotiated on the way back. Look for the large cornices that form along sections of the ridge, making sure not to venture too close to the edge. After passing the intermediate ridge points, start the last haul up the summit ridge with generally moderate scrambling on rock and snow. An ice ax is useful here.

The views from the summit are worth the energy expended to get there. If the wind isn't too strong, the summit makes a great lunch spot. Check out the rugged ridge over to Lenawee Mountain. It looks like a serious undertaking when covered by those huge cornices. Maybe another day?

DESCENT: OK, so you've had a good lunch and are ready to head quickly down to your car. Not so fast! Now those gentle bumps in the ridge that you crossed on the way up look like huge obstacles to be reclimbed on the way down. By the time you have retraced your steps to the ridge intersection at 12,915 feet, you will definitely feel that you've had a workout.

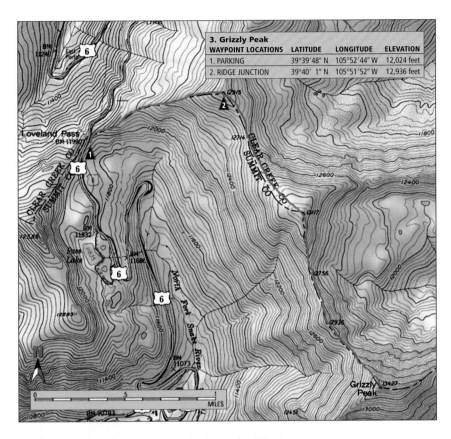

3. Grizzly Peak			
WAYPOINT LOCATIONS	**LATITUDE**	**LONGITUDE**	**ELEVATION**
1. PARKING	39°39'48" N	105°52'44" W	12,024 feet
2. RIDGE JUNCTION	39°40' 1" N	105°51'52" W	12,936 feet

One of the many large cornices that form regularly.

PHOTO BY DAVE COOPER

On the summit ridge of Byers Peak during a CMC trip in February. The cold, windy conditions were good preparation for a climb of Denali later that spring. PHOTO BY DAVE COOPER

4. Byers Peak

ELEVATION GAIN	4,140 feet
ROUND-TRIP DISTANCE	13 miles
STARTING ELEVATION	9,050 feet
HIGHEST ELEVATION	12,804 feet
BEST MONTHS TO CLIMB	January through April
DIFFICULTY	A moderate ski or snowshoe climb on logging roads for the approach, with a steep ski or snowshoe climb (requiring skins if you are on skis) to treeline; a moderate climb to the summit along a corniced ridge with a couple of Class 3 scrambling sections; if you are on skis, the descent from treeline to the road will require advanced telemark or AT technique, since the trees can be quite tight
GEAR	Snowshoes or skis with climbing skins, ice ax
MAP	Bottle Pass 7.5 minute

GETTING THERE: Drive to the town of Frasier, 16.3 miles north of Berthoud Pass on U.S. 40. Turn west at the Conoco station onto Eisenhower Avenue and drive across the tracks. Continue west on Eisenhower to a T-junction, 0.4 mile from U.S. 40. Turn left (south) on Carriage Road and drive just over 0.1 mile to another T-junction. Turn right (west) on County Road 73 (which becomes St. Louis Creek Road). Drive on County Road 73 for 4.4 miles to a well-signed intersection and road closure. Turn right (signed to Byers Peak Trailhead), and drive 0.1 mile to the trailhead parking area. You will pass an information sign for the Frasier Experimental Forest after driving 1.8 miles on County Road 73.

COMMENT: Look to the southwest as you enter the Frasier Valley and one peak dominates the skyline. Standing essentially alone, Byers Peak is not so high—only 12,804 feet—but its isolation contributes to its formidable presence.

In winter, it takes a special effort to climb this peak due to the length of the approach, but an outing here combines several aspects of winter mountaineering—a long approach, best done on skis, a moderate ridge climb with a little scrambling thrown in, and great tree skiing on the descent.

One enjoyable way to do this trip is to camp near the end of the road and make a two-day outing out of it. We used to do this when I led the trip for a number of years for the Colorado Mountain Club. We always had a good time, although on a couple of occasions participants got a little frostnip on their faces while high on the ridge. It's a good place to have a face mask.

APPROACH: From the parking area, head southwest on the signed road to the Byers Peak Trailhead. The road climbs gently for the first 2.9 miles until it reaches the wilderness boundary. In this lower section you will pass three intersections, the first after 0.1 mile, where a road from the Frasier Experimental Station joins from your left. Make sure on the way down to take the fork signed to the parking area. The second intersection, at 0.5 mile, is where the Deadhorse Creek Loop drops down to the right. Stay to the left here, following the signs to the Byers Peak Trail.

At mile 2.0, you'll reach the third junction, where a road signed to the St. Louis Creek Road comes in from your left. Stay straight here and continue to climb to the wilderness boundary at mile 2.9, located at the base of a series of switchbacks. This is the new summer trailhead for the Byers Peak Trail, which continues up the road to your right on a slightly steeper grade.

The road now switchbacks through forest to its end at mile 4.7, indicated only by a small loop. Be sure to stay left on the main road at the top of the first switchback (mile 3.0), where another unsigned road continues straight.

THE CLIMB: From the end of the road, head west and gain the north ridge of Byers some distance south of the Byers Peak—Bottle Peak saddle. Climb south up the ridge through trees, which open up as you gain elevation until you finally reach treeline. This is a good place to leave skis or snowshoes and get out the ice ax. Just make sure that you can find your gear on the descent. Hike south up the ridge, which initially is quite broad but narrows down as you climb higher. The winds create some amazing cornices along this ridge, reminiscent of Alaska. Scramble up the rocky sections and continue to the summit.

DESCENT: Reverse your tracks. The tree skiing back down to the road will test your route finding on skis. Look for the open glades as much as possible, although as you approach the point where you leave the ridge and catch the road, the trees become quite tight. Once you are at the road, head back to the parking area. The switchbacks offer a quick downhill run, followed by a more pedestrian pace on the lower part of the trail. The run down is accomplished in a fraction of the time it took to climb up, which is one reason I prefer skis over snowshoes for this outing.

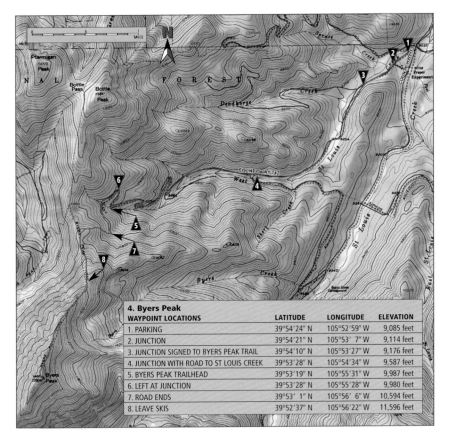

4. Byers Peak			
WAYPOINT LOCATIONS	**LATITUDE**	**LONGITUDE**	**ELEVATION**
1. PARKING	39°54'24" N	105°52'59" W	9,085 feet
2. JUNCTION	39°54'21" N	105°53' 7" W	9,114 feet
3. JUNCTION SIGNED TO BYERS PEAK TRAIL	39°54'10" N	105°53'27" W	9,176 feet
4. JUNCTION WITH ROAD TO ST LOUIS CREEK	39°53'28" N	105°54'34" W	9,587 feet
5. BYERS PEAK TRAILHEAD	39°53'19" N	105°55'31" W	9,987 feet
6. LEFT AT JUNCTION	39°53'28" N	105°55'28" W	9,980 feet
7. ROAD ENDS	39°53' 1" N	105°56' 6" W	10,594 feet
8. LEAVE SKIS	39°52'37" N	105°56'22" W	11,596 feet

Carefully descending one of the rocky steps along the ridge, in windy conditions.

PHOTO BY DAVE COOPER

The 1.3-mile-long ridge to North Star Mountain's true summit offers a good winter workout in a raw, alpine environment.

PHOTO BY DAVE COOPER

5. North Star Mountain—East Ridge

ELEVATION GAIN	2,700 feet
ROUND-TRIP DISTANCE	8.4 miles
STARTING ELEVATION	11,530 feet
HIGHEST ELEVATION	13,614 feet
BEST MONTHS TO CLIMB	December through May
DIFFICULTY	A moderate winter ridge
GEAR	Ice ax, snowshoes
MAPS	Alma 7.5 minute Breckenridge 7.5 minute

GETTING THERE: Drive to Hoosier Pass on Colorado 9. A large parking area is located on the west side of the highway.

COMMENT: Finding quality winter routes with short approaches and reasonable avalanche hazard can sometimes be a challenge. One of my favorites is North Star Mountain. North Star provides a good introduction to winter ridge-running and puts you in a great location, surrounded as it is by high peaks and rugged connecting ridges.

A winter day on the 1.3-mile-long ridge from North Star's false summit to the true summit at the extreme west end of the ridge can be quite a test of your fortitude, not just because you are exposed to the vagaries of winter weather for at least four hours, but also because of the seemingly endless number of ups and downs along the ridge. In the summer months, the ridge flies by, but with the addition of snow, it's a whole different animal, with cornices and tricky sections of snow-covered rock to negotiate. Don't forget that you have to cross the same terrain on the way back.

APPROACH: The traditional approach to the North Star Ridge uses the four-wheel-drive road that heads up from the parking area at Hoosier Pass toward the Magnolia Mine, then cuts up the southeast spur before the closed gate on a social trail. A variation to the road avoids one avalanche-prone slope, 0.9 mile from the pass, by going over the top of the ridge and rejoining the road at a saddle at 12,100 feet.

Recently, questions have been raised about the legality of this approach, since the owners of the Magnolia Mine are the same as those who have caused the closure of the adjacent fourteeners. I hope this will not become

North Star Mountain, viewed from the south side of Hoosier Pass. The broad snow slopes descending towards the camera at the right of this photo are the normal ascent route used to gain the ridge.   PHOTO BY DAVE COOPER

an issue. However, there is another way of approaching the ridge that I believe avoids any problems, so that is the one I will describe here.

From the parking area, head west for a quarter mile to the base of the ski/sledding hill. Turn right (northwest) and contour along the road to Crystal Lake, reached at mile 1.4. Cut over to the ridge north of the lake and follow this ridge to the false summit at 13,430 feet. This route is a little steeper than the normal route, but the difficulty doesn't exceed Class 2.

THE CLIMB: Head west along the ridge, staying close to the crest the whole way. Don't get too close to the edge of any cornices that may form. There are a couple of false summits along the way, but the true summit should be obvious, just before the significant drop to the Wheeler saddle.

DESCENT: Reverse the route.

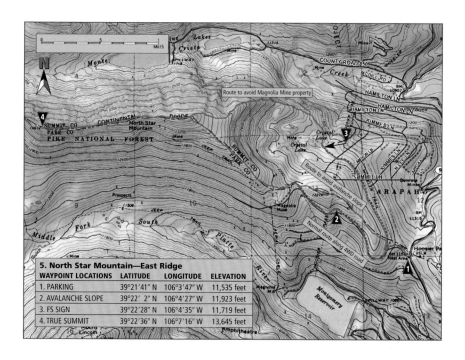

5. North Star Mountain—East Ridge			
WAYPOINT LOCATIONS	LATITUDE	LONGITUDE	ELEVATION
1. PARKING	39°21'41" N	106°3'47" W	11,535 feet
2. AVALANCHE SLOPE	39°22' 2" N	106°4'27" W	11,923 feet
3. FS SIGN	39°22'28" N	106°4'35" W	11,719 feet
4. TRUE SUMMIT	39°22'36" N	106°7'16" W	13,645 feet

Heading up to the ridge with the slopes of Mount Lincoln in the distance.

PHOTO BY DAVE COOPER

The east ridge of Mount Bancroft offers a fine winter mountaineering challenge, with knife-edge snow ridges and rock scrambling from Class 3 through 5.2. PHOTO BY KEVIN CRAIG

6. Mount Bancroft—East Ridge

ELEVATION GAIN	3,030 feet
ROUND-TRIP DISTANCE	7.9 miles
STARTING ELEVATION	10,360 feet
HIGHEST ELEVATION	13,250 feet
BEST MONTHS TO CLIMB	December through May
DIFFICULTY	A steep snow and rock ridge with one rappel, a short pitch of 5.2 rock, and much Class 3 and 4 scrambling
GEAR	Crampons, ice ax, snowshoes, and helmet; 150-foot rope required for the rappel, plus a few medium pieces of rock pro to protect the climb out of the notch
MAP	Empire 7.5 minute

GETTING THERE: Take the Fall River Road exit from Interstate 70 (exit 238). Head north on this paved road for 8.3 miles. Turn left onto Alice Road, and after one mile, turn right onto Stewart Road (Forest Service Road 701.2). During the winter, Stewart Road is not plowed. Usually a small parking area big enough for two vehicles is provided at the start of the road. Later in the spring it may be possible to drive at least partway to Loch Lomond. Two gates along this road, also known as the Loch Lomond Road, are closed during the winter and spring months. Specifically, the lower gate is closed from December 1 to June 1, while the upper gate is closed from October 15 to July 15.

COMMENT: Many climbers might argue that the most serious objective hazard on this route is the wind. Especially in winter, the winds have turned around many parties, so this route typically has a lower success rate than some of the other winter ridge routes described in this guide. Although much of the route has difficulties comparable to those found on Torrey's Kelso ridge, Bancroft's notch, with its rappel and subsequent climb back out, boosts this route into the technical realm. Choose a day when the winds are predicted to be moderate and you'll be rewarded with a fine mountaineering route with a bit of everything. Expect to find the route at its snowiest in April.

APPROACH: Follow Stewart Road initially west, then curve to the north as it nears Loch Lomond at mile 2.2. Snow conditions will dictate the route to gain the east ridge, to the west of the lake.

The author enjoying the short, technical rock pitch immediately after the rappel.

THE CLIMB: The ridge starts out with moderate rocky slopes. It gradually steepens and narrows until you reach the notch in the ridge at 12,300 feet. Most parties choose to rappel into the notch in the summer. With snow on the route, the rappel becomes mandatory. A 150-foot rope makes it with a few feet to spare. Don't trust old slings. They are frequently gnawed on by small critters. Once you are in the notch, you may have a few choices to climb out of the west side. In the summer it is relatively straightforward to go either left or right on Class 4 terrain, but snow can make these options less attractive. It might be best to plan on climbing the crack system in the center of the face (5.2). With snow- and ice-covered ledges and wet boots, it is advisable to leave the rope out for this short section.

Continue up the ridge along nice knife-edge snow ridges alternating with rock towers requiring some Class 4 moves. Typically, the snow dictates staying on the ridge crest, increasing the difficulty over a summer excursion. Continuously interesting climbing with sometimes complex route finding brings you to the top of the ridge at 13,000 feet. From here it is a short walk to the summit of Bancroft.

DESCENT: Walk down the gentle southeast ridge or, in the spring, glissade the slopes to the vicinity of Lake Caroline before rejoining the road for the walk back to the car.

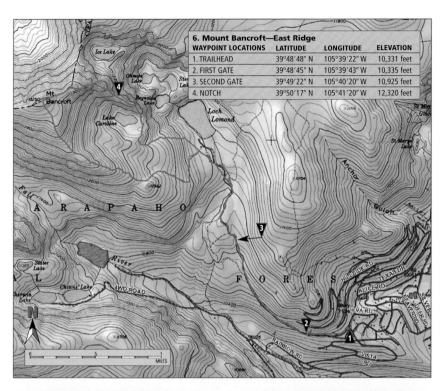

6. Mount Bancroft—East Ridge			
WAYPOINT LOCATIONS	LATITUDE	LONGITUDE	ELEVATION
1. TRAILHEAD	39°48'48" N	105°39'22" W	10,331 feet
2. FIRST GATE	39°48'45" N	105°39'43" W	10,335 feet
3. SECOND GATE	39°49'22" N	105°40'20" W	10,925 feet
4. NOTCH	39°50'17" N	105°41'20" W	12,320 feet

Clouds clearing from Mount Bancroft and James Peak on a crisp winter morning.

Martha rises above a frozen Chasm Lake. The route offers four to five pitches of roped climbing, with everything from steep snow to ice to moderate mixed climbing.

7. Mount Lady Washington— Martha Couloir

ELEVATION GAIN	3,940 feet
ROUND-TRIP DISTANCE	8.4 miles
STARTING ELEVATION	9,450 feet
HIGHEST ELEVATION	13,281 feet
BEST MONTHS TO CLIMB	December through May
DIFFICULTY	Steep snow, 5.0 rock through M3, depending on conditions
GEAR	Two ice tools, crampons, rope, alpine rock rack, a couple of ice screws, helmet
MAP	Longs Peak 7.5 minute

GETTING THERE: Drive north from Lyons on Colorado 7 from its junction with U.S. 36 for 25.1 miles, or go south on Colorado 7 for 9.2 miles from its intersection with U.S. 36 in Estes Park. Turn west at the sign for Longs Peak Area and drive 1.1 miles to park at the Longs Peak Ranger Station. Rocky Mountain National Park fees are not collected at this location.

COMMENT: A climb that has become quite popular in recent years, Martha faces Dreamweaver on the north side of Chasm Lake. Shorter but with similar climbing to Dreamweaver, the route usually forms much earlier than its neighbor and is gone by the time Dreamweaver comes into shape in the spring. With its southern exposure, conditions can change rapidly from mostly snow to a mix of snow and ice and back again, but the route tends to be climbable for much of the winter and early spring as long as avalanche conditions are reasonable. This is another transitional climb; although it is primarily a snow route, it provides an opportunity to combine snow climbing with ice and mixed climbing for those who wish to advance their skills in that direction.

On one occasion, we were climbing Martha in late-season conditions when the climb was pretty much "out of shape," making the cruxes more difficult than usual (less ice, lots of wet rock). A rock the size of a microwave oven came tumbling down the climb, narrowly missing us. When conditions are that marginal, it is probably better to stay away because, with so much melting going on, you should expect more rockfall.

The third pitch in lean conditions.
PHOTO BY DAVE COOPER

APPROACH: From the parking area at the ranger station, follow the Longs Peak Trail to Chasm Lake for 4.2 miles (staying left at the Granite Pass turnoff), until the trail peters out in a meadow by the ranger hut. Scramble west up to Chasm Lake and traverse right on large, unstable boulders to the base of the climb, a deeply inset gully halfway around the north side of the lake. If the lake is well frozen, walk straight across the ice and scramble up the boulders to the base of the climb.

THE CLIMB: The climb is normally done in four to five pitches. The first pitch heads up moderate snow slopes to a short, easy rock and ice step, then continues up to a belay on the right. Depending on where you rope up, this pitch could be longer than a rope length and may require some simul-climbing. The second pitch continues up a snow rib to a belay stance on the right side, just before the gully narrows to a few feet in width. Pitch three climbs the narrow slot to another constriction with an iced-up step near the top. Look for a fixed pin on the left for a belay. In lean conditions, this can be tricky to surmount. Head up the fourth pitch on snow and mixed terrain and reach another crux, an iced-up rock step. After this, the difficulties are at an end. Climb up moderate snow and talus slopes to the summit as the gully widens. This can be a tedious section.

DESCENT: The most direct descent is via the east ridge of Mount Lady Washington back to the Chasm Lake trail junction. From here, follow the Longs Peak Trail down to the parking area.

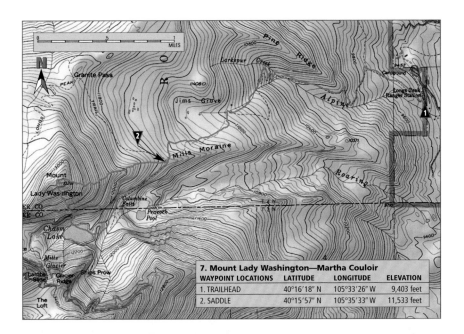

7. Mount Lady Washington—Martha Couloir			
WAYPOINT LOCATIONS	**LATITUDE**	**LONGITUDE**	**ELEVATION**
1. TRAILHEAD	40°16'18" N	105°33'26" W	9,403 feet
2. SADDLE	40°15'57" N	105°35'33" W	11,533 feet

Climbing one of the mixed cruxes.

The approach to Chasm View provides dramatic views of the Diamond. The north face route climbs the rock and snow immediately to the right of the Diamond.

8. Longs Peak—
North Face (Cables Route)

ELEVATION GAIN	4,850 feet
ROUND-TRIP DISTANCE	12.2 miles
STARTING ELEVATION	9,450 feet
HIGHEST ELEVATION	14,267 feet
BEST MONTHS TO CLIMB	December through May, although the best snow conditions may be found in the spring
DIFFICULTY	One pitch of 5.4 rock climbing that may be dry, iced over, or covered with snow; steep snow
GEAR	Crampons, ice tools, small alpine rock rack, and possibly a picket or two; two ropes are required for the rappel unless you use the intermediate eyebolts
MAP	Longs Peak 7.5 minute

GETTING THERE: Drive north from Lyons on Colorado 7 from its junction with U.S. 36 for 25.1 miles or go south on Colorado 7 for 9.2 miles from its intersection with U.S. 36 in Estes Park. Turn west at the sign for Longs Peak Area and drive 1.1 miles to park at the Longs Peak Ranger Station. Rocky Mountain National Park fees are not collected at this location.

COMMENT: An absolute classic, the Cables Route in winter has long been a rite of passage for mountaineers. The jet stream seems to target this peak for much of the winter, so it is the rare day that sees calm conditions. More often than not, climbers come back with stories of being blown off their feet in the Boulder Field (if they get that far). On those occasions when weather conditions are favorable, you might find good snow conditions, dry rock on the Cables section, or, more likely, verglas-covered rock. So, while the route is a worthwhile test in winter, the best snow conditions are likely to be experienced in the spring, after a few of the large dumps of snow characteristic of this time of year. No matter which of these seasons you choose to climb this route, you will be treated to a magnificent location and a climb with a very alpine feel.

APPROACH: Yes, once again it's the long slog up the Longs Peak Trail. How well you come to know the early-morning starts, your world defined by the edge of the headlamp beam, walking up the well-trodden snow- and ice-covered trail, often to reach treeline just as the sun lightens the eastern sky.

Climbers on the crux mixed pitch.

PHOTO BY DAVE COOPER

How many times will you grab for the camera as sunrise bathes the peaks in an intense pink glow?

From the Longs Peak Trailhead, start up the well-signed Longs Peak Trail. Often, when snow-covered, the track deviates slightly from the summer trail just below treeline. Where the maintained trail crosses to the south side of Alpine Brook, after 1.9 miles at 10,600 feet, a well-trodden path heads west directly up the drainage and rejoins the regular trail in a quarter mile. On some occasions, both paths have been tracked, which means that things can get a little confusing, especially on the way down. Take careful note of your route so that you are able to retrace your steps on your return. After rejoining the maintained trail, pass the turnoff to Jims Grove and continue as the trail wanders up onto the Mills Moraine, reaching the Chasm Lake Trail junction at 11,530 feet, 3.0 miles from the trailhead. The solar outhouse makes this spot difficult to miss.

This time you head over Granite Pass to the Boulder Field. Sometimes you can follow the summer trail, and other times you must navigate around the broad shoulder of Mount Lady Washington. As you gain the Boulder

Field, the north face and the top of the Diamond come into view—always enough to take your breath away.

THE CLIMB: Aim for the base of the route, located directly above Chasm View. A steep snow slope takes you up to the technical pitch. Sometimes the old eyebolts (relics of the cable) are wanded. The pitch goes up a right-facing corner. Rock pro can be placed on the wall to your left, plus the eyebolts appear to be bombproof. A tricky move at just over 30 meters gets you to the top eyebolt. Note its location for the rappel. It is possible to reach a rock anchor at exactly 60 meters, but with a 60-meter rope, this requires your partner to simul-climb a few feet. In April 2007, a fixed stopper was located in a crack in this rock. Back it up. Depending on snow conditions, it may be worth leaving the rope out for a bit as you choose a route up the snow from here, possibly simul-climbing if the snow is suspect. There are usually several possibilities. A good route goes directly up from the rock mentioned to hit the northwest ridge a little below the summit.

DESCENT: Reverse the route, making at least one double-rope rappel, from the top eyebolt.

A stormy day on the north face.

Climbing above the Cables section.

PHOTO BY DAVE COOPER

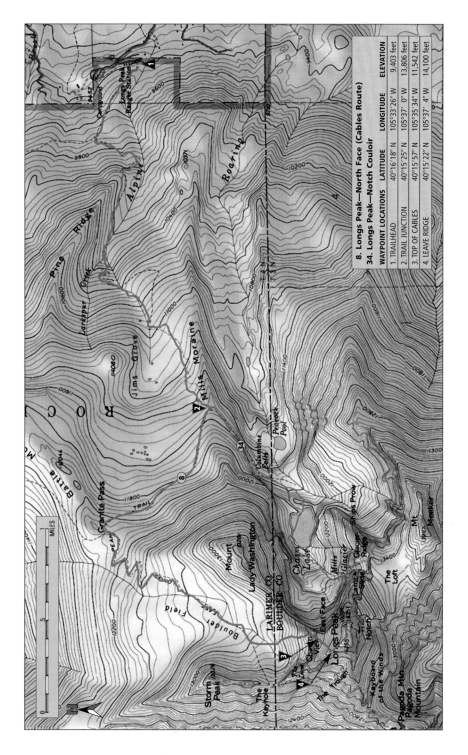

WAYPOINT LOCATIONS	LATITUDE	LONGITUDE	ELEVATION
1. TRAILHEAD	40°16'18" N	105°33'26" W	9,403 feet
2. TRAIL JUNCTION	40°15'25" N	105°37' 0" W	13,806 feet
3. TOP OF CABLES	40°15'57" N	105°35'34" W	11,542 feet
4. LEAVE RIDGE	40°15'22" N	105°37' 4" W	14,100 feet

8. Longs Peak—North Face (Cables Route)

34. Longs Peak—Notch Couloir

The aesthetic summit ridge on Mount Guyot features large cornices and an exposed finish along a knife-edge snow ridge.

9. Mount Guyot—Southeast Ridge

ELEVATION GAIN	2,500 feet
ROUND-TRIP DISTANCE	4.2 miles, plus any distance walked along the road
STARTING ELEVATION	10,814 feet
HIGHEST ELEVATION	13,370 feet
BEST MONTHS TO CLIMB	April through mid June
DIFFICULTY	Moderate snow climbing, but with an exposed and possibly corniced summit ridge
GEAR	Ice ax, snowshoes or skis
MAP	Boreas Pass 7.5 minute

GETTING THERE: From the town of Jefferson, head north on County Road 35, signed as Jefferson Lake Rd. and Michigan Creek Rd. After 2.1 miles, go straight at the T-junction. At 2.9 miles, bear right on County Road 54. At 5.4 miles, County Road 54 turns left, signed to Georgia Pass. Drive past the Michigan Creek Campground and keep going for a total of 10.0 miles from Jefferson to a point where a clearing allows access to Guyot's southeast ridge. It is also possible to continue on the road for another 0.5 mile to where an old logging road takes off to the west. Following this logging road will eventually bring you back onto the southeast ridge at 11,200 feet. Note: How far you can drive up the road toward Georgia Pass is determined by the snowdrifts and your vehicle. By late May, the road is sometimes drivable all the way to the starting point for the climb.

COMMENT: Mount Guyot is the prominent peak seen at the edge of South Park as you descend from Kenosha Pass. It is characterized by a sweeping ridge with large cornices visible in the winter and spring. Spring is my favorite time of year to climb this peak, and the southeast ridge is the best route, offering a moderate snow climb with a kick in the tail—a narrow, corniced, knife-edged ridge to the summit. In early May, the approach and lower part of the ridge offer excellent skiing, but by late May, snowshoes may be preferred, since the snow on the lower ridge is no longer continuous. After mid June, the snow will be largely gone. Get an early start to take advantage of the firmer snow.

APPROACH: The approach consists of the section of road you are unable to drive because of snowdrifts. This can be anywhere from nothing to several miles.

Mount Guyot is seen at the right in this view from South Park. The southeast ridge faces the camera in this photo.   PHOTO BY DAVE COOPER

THE CLIMB: Make your way northwest up the initially gentle ridge, picking the line of least resistance through the trees. At treeline, climb up a steeper snow slope for 200 feet, at which point the slope flattens out for several hundred yards before starting up in earnest. There is some avalanche potential on the broad, lower slopes. Choose a route that avoids any avalanche danger. Often this is the ridgeline on the right margin of the slope. Climb north on moderate snow to join the east ridge at 13,000 feet. The final section of the ridge, up to the summit, can be heavily corniced, so be careful not to get too close to the edge. This final section of the ridge, with its cornices and knife-edged sections, makes this route great training for those planning to head down to South America for some of the moderate but high routes to be found in Bolivia and Peru.

DESCENT: The descent consists of glissades and plunge-stepping back down the way you came up. You may not need snowshoes until below treeline. If you have skis along, well....

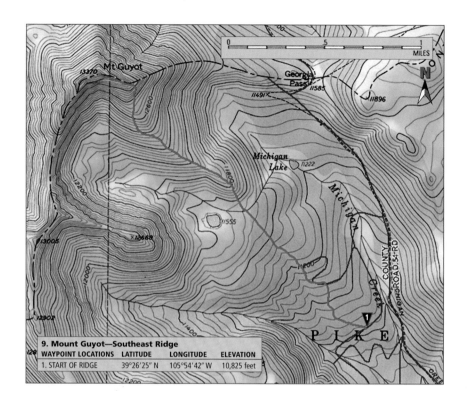

9. Mount Guyot—Southeast Ridge			
WAYPOINT LOCATIONS	LATITUDE	LONGITUDE	ELEVATION
1. START OF RIDGE	39°26'25" N	105°54'42" W	10,825 feet

High on the ridge.

Climbers approaching Fletcher's summit via the moderate southeast ridge. The climber in the foreground is rounding the head of the couloir described in climb #23.

10. Fletcher Mountain— Southeast Ridge

ELEVATION GAIN	3,100 feet
ROUND-TRIP DISTANCE	8.0 miles
STARTING ELEVATION	10,900 feet
HIGHEST ELEVATION	13,951 feet
BEST MONTHS TO CLIMB	April through June
DIFFICULTY	Moderate snow climbing with some exposure on the final summit ridge
GEAR	Ice ax, snowshoes, or skis with climbing skins
MAPS	Breckenridge 7.5 minute Copper Mountain 7.5 minute

GETTING THERE: When you are 7.6 miles south of Breckenridge on Colorado 9, or 2.3 miles north of Hoosier Pass on Colorado 9, turn west on Blue Lakes Road (dirt) and drive as far as the road is plowed, often 0.3 mile from the highway. Park in the plowed-out area, being careful not to block access to the homes in the area.

COMMENT: This snow climb is another favorite and one that I have used many times to introduce mountaineering students to the fun of climbing snow ridges. The southeast summit ridge on Fletcher Mountain offers a very nice, knife-edge snow-climbing experience.

A bonus for this outing is that the ski mountaineering can be outstanding, with many options for ski descents, from moderate slopes to somewhat steeper lines. Often in late April a long section of the flats below the summit can be bare of snow, and snowshoes may be a better option. Sometimes May snowstorms will fill in these sections, allowing you to stay on snow for almost the entire outing.

APPROACH: Hike west up the Blue Lakes Road from the parking area toward the reservoir. How far up this road you are able to drive will depend on the snow conditions. It is usually plowed to at least Quandary's Monte Cristo Trailhead, 0.3 mile from Colorado 9. From this parking area, it is 1.8 miles to the reservoir, under the looming mass of Quandary Peak. When you reach the reservoir, scramble up a short, gravelly trail to the right of the dam and continue walking along the north side of the reservoir for approximately 0.1 mile until a suitable snow slope allows you to begin a rising traverse. You

Climbers can be seen approaching Fletcher's summit block.

will head northwest toward a relatively flat area at 12,200 feet. From this flat area you have two options—continue straight and climb the nose of the ridge directly west, or head up the valley to the northwest, going generally toward the saddle between Fletcher Mountain and Quandary Peak, then exiting left onto the flats below Fletcher. This valley contains snow well into late spring and has significant avalanche potential. It is best to avoid it unless conditions are stable. The normal route heads up the nose of the ridge. It is initially steep but moderates as it swings to the northwest and finally deposits you on the large plateau leading to Fletcher. From here, the route to Fletcher's summit is clearly visible. Head northwest across the plateau to gain the southeast ridge of Fletcher at around 13,400 feet.

THE CLIMB: The actual line you take will depend on snow conditions, but generally stay close to or on the ridge for the remaining 550 feet of climbing. This usually involves a mixture of snow and talus until you are on the ridge proper. Here it narrows dramatically, occasionally forming a cornice, but it almost always ends in a knife-edge near the summit.

DESCENT: If you are on skis, you will choose a suitable line to ski. Otherwise, follow your steps back down to the parking area.

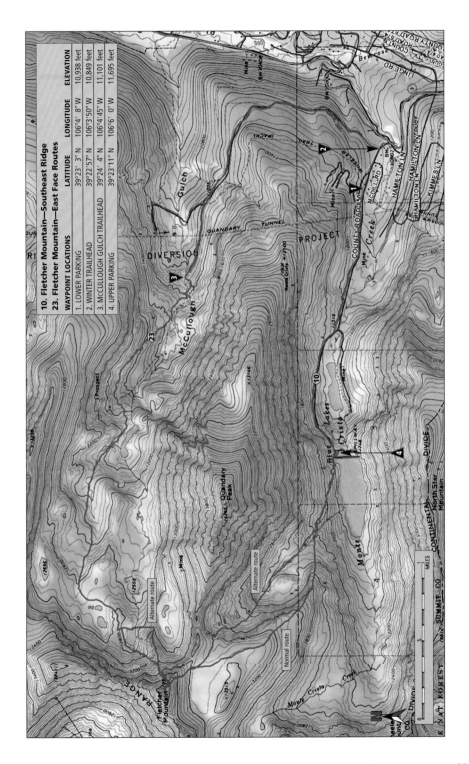

WAYPOINT LOCATIONS	LATITUDE	LONGITUDE	ELEVATION
1. LOWER PARKING	39°23′ 3″ N	106°4′ 8″ W	10,938 feet
2. WINTER TRAILHEAD	39°22′57″ N	106°3′50″ W	10,849 feet
3. McCULLOUGH GULCH TRAILHEAD	39°24′ 4″ N	106°4′45″ W	11,101 feet
4. UPPER PARKING	39°23′11″ N	106°6′ 0″ W	11,695 feet

10. Fletcher Mountain—Southeast Ridge
23. Fletcher Mountain—East Face Routes

This dramatic view of the Cristo couloir is taken from North Star Mountain, and clearly shows two of the starts that are possible to gain the upper snowfield. PHOTO BY KEVIN CRAIG

11. Quandary Peak—
South Couloir (Cristo Couloir)

ELEVATION GAIN	2,550 feet
ROUND-TRIP DISTANCE	2.3 miles if you descend the couloir, 4.2 miles if you descend the east-ridge route (plus, unless you bring two vehicles, you'll have to walk back up Blue Lakes Road to your vehicle, adding 2.4 miles and 870 feet of elevation gain)
STARTING ELEVATION	11,700 feet
HIGHEST ELEVATION	14,265 feet
BEST MONTHS TO CLIMB	Mid April to mid June; later in the season, expect a short section of scree, easily negotiated, near the top
DIFFICULTY	Moderate snow
GEAR	Crampons, ice ax, helmet, and snowshoes if descending the east-ridge route
MAP	Breckenridge 7.5 minute

GETTING THERE: When you are 7.6 miles south of Breckenridge on Colorado 9, or 2.3 miles north of Hoosier Pass on Colorado 9, turn west on Blue Lakes Road (dirt) and drive 2.2 miles west to a parking area by the dam. In May, the road probably won't be open all the way, so park in a suitable spot and walk the road to the dam.

COMMENT: A rite of spring, I usually head up this climb every year. With a short approach and fun climbing, it is a good way to shake off the cobwebs. With an early start, the firm snow can be ideal for crampon practice and is used for this purpose by many schools. It is also used as an introduction to snow and couloir climbing. The couloir provides almost 2,500 feet of moderate snow climbing.

APPROACH: Assuming that you are able to drive to the parking area by the dam, the approach is short and sweet. Scramble up the loose trail to the top of the dam, then drop down the other side and walk 0.1 mile west to the base of the first prominent gully.

THE CLIMB: Several variations are available to start the route. The most direct is to head up the first gully west of the dam, but look for other possibilities, some of which offer steeper climbing. Assuming you start up

Mountaineering students practicing roped team travel.

the first gully past the dam, head up for perhaps 100 yards and then traverse left (west) into the next gully to continue heading up. The couloir (really more of a shallow drift gully formed on the lee side of a rock rib) averages around 30 degrees, although short sections will approach 45 degrees. A scree band near the top is easily negotiated by heading to the right a short distance until you can again head up. The summit usually has a few waves of snow that can make the last few feet fun.

DESCENT: If the snow is still in good shape, the descent down the route is quick and fun. If snow conditions aren't to your liking, the east-ridge route is a good alternative, but longer.

To follow the east ridge down, stay on the ridge crest to treeline. (The summer trail isn't a good option in winter or spring because it is routed through and under cornices that form regularly.) With snow on the ridge, the summer trail is hard to find below treeline. This means that some route finding below treeline will be necessary unless there is already a track. From the summer trailhead, hike south back to Blue Lakes Road and then west on the road back to your vehicle.

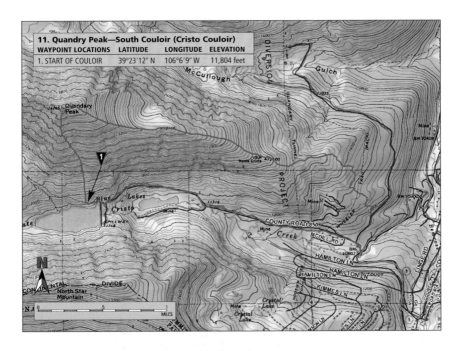

11. Quandry Peak—South Couloir (Cristo Couloir)			
WAYPOINT LOCATIONS	LATITUDE	LONGITUDE	ELEVATION
1. START OF COULOIR	39°23′12″ N	106°6′9″ W	11,804 feet

Heading up the lower slopes of the couloir, with the dam below.

PHOTO BY DAVE COOPER

This view from the upper lake shows the direct line above the lake. Several other lower angle routes are possible to the right, one of which will be used on the descent.   PHOTO BY DAVE COOPER

12. Wheeler Mountain

ELEVATION GAIN	2,900 feet
ROUND-TRIP DISTANCE	9.0 miles
STARTING ELEVATION	10,890 feet
HIGHEST ELEVATION	13,690 feet
BEST MONTHS TO CLIMB	April through mid June
DIFFICULTY	An approach along a four-wheel-drive road, with a moderate snow climb to a rough Class 4 ridge that may be technical when snow-covered
GEAR	Ice ax and possibly crampons; a rope could be useful for the summit ridge when it is snow-covered
MAPS	Alma 7.5 minute Climax 7.5 minute Copper Mountain 7.5 minute

GETTING THERE: One mile south of Hoosier Pass on Colorado 9, take the sharp exit west onto Park County Road 4. Follow Park County Road 4 downhill, staying straight on it after 0.8 mile where Nuthatch Drive makes a sharp turn to the left. In 0.2 mile after this junction, you will come to a three-way junction. Park County Road 4 turns sharply to the left, while the middle fork continues slightly downhill to the Montgomery Reservoir Dam. Take the right fork (Forest Service Road 408), which passes through an open gate and contours above the reservoir to a parking area by the spillway, a total of 1.6 miles from Colorado 9. Later in the spring, the gate is open and it is possible to park approximately one third of a mile farther along. A little before the Magnolia Mill the road becomes very rough.

COMMENT: The upper basin of the Middle Fork of the South Platte River tends to hold snow well into late spring and often early summer, providing many opportunities for snow climbs.

One of my favorites is Wheeler Peak via Wheeler Lake. When the spring snow has consolidated, the climb up to the south ridge of Wheeler from the lower lake can be a good, moderate snow climb. The route along the ridge to the summit of Wheeler should only be attempted by experienced climbers, especially if it is snow covered.

APPROACH: From the parking area, head southwest on the road as it contours around to the west end of the lake, and go through a closed gate. The road heads up the valley, passing under the Magnolia Mill. Stay away

Looking back down the route. Both lakes can be seen below.

PHOTO BY DAVE COOPER

from the buildings, which are privately owned and are currently undergoing some repairs. After passing the mill, the jeep trail stays to the right of the drainage to avoid private property (and also to avoid the willows filling the bottom of the valley). After 2.9 miles, the road starts to diagonal up the right hand side of the valley toward the lake and should be obvious. Follow the road as it climbs until snow slopes allow you to head directly toward the lake, avoiding some potential avalanche slopes just west of the road.

THE CLIMB: Contour around the left side of the lower lake, and follow the drainage from the upper lake, usually staying to the left (west) of the drainage itself. (There is a very real danger in the spring of falling through a snow bridge into these fast-flowing streams, which then go back under the snow, making an exit next to impossible.) Also, stay clear of the potential avalanche paths coming off of the shoulder of Clinton Peak. From the upper lake, the steepest snow line climbs left of the lake and up a finger of snow to a flatter area. Once you reach this flatter area, decide on your route: Either angle left toward the Clinton-Wheeler saddle, or, if snow conditions are good, head up a steeper (approximately 40-degree) snow slope to the right, aiming for the first ridge point to the right (north) of the saddle. From here, the route will depend on snow conditions. A climbers' trail of sorts stays slightly west of the ridgeline, but this may not be a good choice when covered in snow. Staying on the ridge crest requires some Class 4 scrambling when conditions are dry; with snow, a rope might be useful. The short distance from the Clinton-Wheeler saddle to the summit of Wheeler Mountain can be slow going on this quite challenging terrain.

DESCENT: To descend, head back to the saddle, then pick a route back down (the exact route chosen will depend on how soft the snow has become).

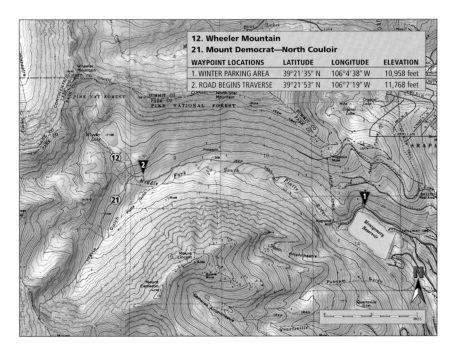

12. Wheeler Mountain			
21. Mount Democrat—North Couloir			
WAYPOINT LOCATIONS	LATITUDE	LONGITUDE	ELEVATION
1. WINTER PARKING AREA	39°21′35″ N	106°4′38″ W	10,958 feet
2. ROAD BEGINS TRAVERSE	39°21′53″ N	106°7′19″ W	11,768 feet

The summit ridge on Wheeler in lean conditions. Snow can add to the challenge on this section of the route.

This photo, one of my favorites, from the first time I climbed Castle Peak back in the early 1990s, shows the fun snow ridge below the summit.   PHOTO BY CHARLIE WINGER

13. Castle Peak—Northeast Ridge

ELEVATION GAIN	4,500 feet
ROUND-TRIP DISTANCE	10.9 miles
STARTING ELEVATION	9,750 feet
HIGHEST ELEVATION	14,265 feet
BEST MONTHS TO CLIMB	May and June; early in May there can still be significant avalanche danger
DIFFICULTY	A simple snow climb to a ridge; the final climb on the summit ridge is often airy, with hard-packed snow, requiring care
GEAR	Ice ax and crampons, snowshoes or skis
MAPS	Pearl Pass 7.5 minute Hayden Peak 7.5 minute

GETTING THERE: From the large roundabout on U.S. 82 at the north end of Aspen, take the Castle Creek Road (signed to Ashcroft) for 13.0 miles to the road closure. The Pearl Pass Road takes off to the right and is well signed.

COMMENT: A climb that I never get tired of returning to, this route is little more than a straightforward snow walk at high altitude. Yet the location makes it, for me, one of the more aesthetic routes in this guidebook. The Montezuma Basin is an amazing place during the spring, surrounded by rugged peaks and endless snowfields. Once you are on the northeast ridge of Castle, you are rewarded with great views. The glissade from the saddle between Castle and Conundrum peaks is one of the better ones to be found. In short, this route can get a newcomer to snow climbing hooked on the sport, while experienced mountaineers will simply enjoy a mellow outing in a beautiful setting. If the Pearl Pass Road is well covered by snow, skis provide the ideal flotation for the approach to the upper basin. Otherwise, it would be wise to carry snowshoes for the softer snow conditions often found on the descent.

APPROACH: From the start of the Pearl Pass Road at the road closure, follow the road through trees and the occasional clearing as it gradually climbs into the upper part of Castle Creek, passing dispersed camping sites around the 1 mile mark. At mile 1.3, the road crosses Castle Creek on a bridge and continues to head southwest, now on the south side of the creek.

The road passes several avalanche chutes on the northwest face of Greg Mace Peak as you gain elevation. After 2.8 miles, you will reach the road

The route heads up Montezuma Basin (lower left), then left into the valley between Castle and Conundrum before gaining the northeast ridge, seen on the skyline.   PHOTO BY DAVE COOPER

junction where the road into Montezuma Basin takes off to the right. Leave the Pearl Pass Road here and contour north on the road as it enters Montezuma Basin.

THE CLIMB: Before crossing the open slopes below Malamute Peak, make sure that the avalanche hazard is reasonable, and remember that you will be recrossing these slopes on your return later in the day. Having been here in the winter, I can attest to the fact that this can be a downright scary place in that season and best avoided during times of high avalanche danger. The road, possibly visible in a few spots where the wind has scoured off the snow, makes a rising traverse across these slopes on its way to the Montezuma Mine. Generally, follow the road until the basin curves around to the west, rising in a series of broad benches until you reach the impressive bowl between Castle and Conundrum at 13,470 feet. Look for a trail that cuts back to your left and then climbs gradually to meet the northeast ridge at a saddle at 13,750 feet. The trail tends to be blown clear in places, so it shouldn't be too difficult to locate. Once you are on the ridge, head south-west on snow and rock, occasionally encountering a brief section of Class 3 scrambling that can be tricky if there is a thin layer of fresh snow. The final short section of the ridge offers a great finish to the climb on a narrow snow ridge, usually of hard-packed snow that may require crampons.

DESCENT: Either reverse your track down the northeast ridge, or head down Castle's straightforward northwest ridge to the Castle-Conundrum saddle. When conditions are good, the glissade from this saddle into the upper bowl is excellent, although I've seen inexperienced climbers tumbling out of control down this slope. This isn't the place to learn how to use an ice ax.

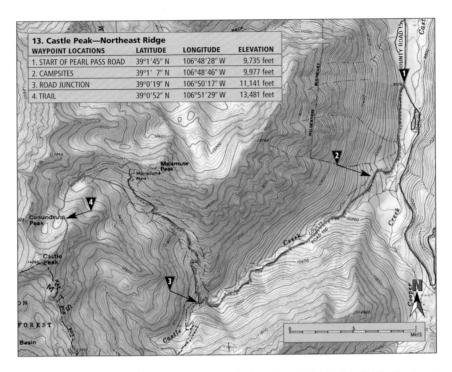

| 13. Castle Peak—Northeast Ridge | | | |
WAYPOINT LOCATIONS	LATITUDE	LONGITUDE	ELEVATION
1. START OF PEARL PASS ROAD	39°1′45″ N	106°48′28″ W	9,735 feet
2. CAMPSITES	39°1′ 7″ N	106°48′46″ W	9,977 feet
3. ROAD JUNCTION	39°0′19″ N	106°50′17″ W	11,141 feet
4. TRAIL	39°0′52″ N	106°51′29″ W	13,481 feet

Sunrise over Malamute Peak, from high in Montezuma Basin.

PHOTO BY DAVE COOPER

The northeast face and east ridge of Niagara Peak, seen from Jones Mountain. The narrow couloir at lower right provides access to the face.

PHOTO BY DAVE COOPER

14. Niagara Peak—
Northeast Face and East Ridge

ELEVATION GAIN	3,050 feet
ROUND-TRIP DISTANCE	6.2 miles
STARTING ELEVATION	10,767 feet
HIGHEST ELEVATION	13,807 feet
BEST MONTHS TO CLIMB	May and June
DIFFICULTY	Your choice of a snow face and gully system or a nice sharp snow ridge with some exposure
GEAR	Ice ax and crampons; snowshoes may be necessary on the approach
MAP	Handies Peak 7.5 minute

GETTING THERE: Drive to the town of Silverton on U.S. 550. Turn onto Silverton's main street (County Road 2) and drive northeast through the town for 0.9 mile to a junction. Stay right on County Road 2. When you are 2.9 miles from the junction of County Road 2 and U.S. 550, the pavement ends and becomes a good gravel road. Pass through Howardsville at 5.1 miles and the old mining town of Eureka at 8.8 miles. You'll reach a point at 11.7 miles where County Road 2 crosses to the east side of the Animas River. Parking spots are available close to this point.

COMMENT: The east ridge and northeast face of Niagara Peak are among my favorite moderate snow climbs. Often overlooked by climbers intent on scaling their better-known neighbors, this peak puts you into the heart of the San Juan Range and provides excellent views of the surrounding terrain. All in a half-day climb!

Climbing the northeast face and descending the east ridge makes a nice tour. While you're up there, you may also want to make the straightforward climb of Jones Mountain, a ranked "Centennial" peak, by its south ridge.

By the way, as you hike up Burns Gulch, you are looking at the north face of Niagara. The northeast face is out of sight to the left and isn't visible until you are high in the basin.

Burns Gulch is threatened by avalanche hazard from both sides. Wait for stable snow conditions before heading up there.

APPROACH: From the bridge, follow the jeep road on the east side of the Animas River. This close to its source, the river is quite modest compared to

High on the northeast face.

the major geographic feature it becomes further downstream. Continue on this road as it climbs gently, crossing the outflow from Grouse Gulch after about 200 yards. At a quarter mile, the jeep road forks; take the left fork (the right fork only parallels the Animas River). As the jeep road gradually rises, it curves around to the southeast and enters Burns Gulch, a spectacular high valley. Continue on the road as it crosses the creek at 11,800 feet, passing several old mines. Later in the spring and summer, it may be possible to stay on the road to 12,100 feet, but when the basin is filled with snow, just head up the gentle snowfields toward the obvious saddle separating Jones and Niagara. A social trail just below the saddle can help in negotiating a small cliff band.

THE CLIMB: Turn right at the saddle and head up the fine knife-edge snow ridge that forms reliably each year. Six hundred feet of climbing will bring you to Niagara's summit.

Another option is to directly climb the snowfields on the northeast face of Niagara. These allow direct access to the summit and offer 800 feet of moderate snow climbing averaging 33 degrees, although you will encounter sections up to 45 degrees in steepness. Start by climbing a narrow snow gully between rock formations, which is highly visible as you approach the head of the valley. As you exit this gully, the snowfields of the northeast face open above you. The summit offers views of the Grenadier and Needles ranges, as well as the nearby fourteeners—Handies, Sunshine, Redcloud, Wetterhorn, and Uncompahgre, to name but a few.

DESCENT: Descend the east ridge back to the saddle and then to the trailhead.

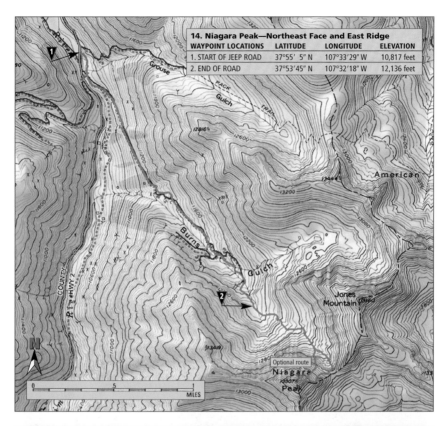

14. Niagara Peak—Northeast Face and East Ridge			
WAYPOINT LOCATIONS	LATITUDE	LONGITUDE	ELEVATION
1. START OF JEEP ROAD	37°55′ 5″ N	107°33′29″ W	10,817 feet
2. END OF ROAD	37°53′45″ N	107°32′18″ W	12,136 feet

Approaching the narrow couloir that provides the most direct route to gain the northeast face.

PHOTO BY DAVE COOPER

Dramatic morning light on the Dragons Tail Couloir. Both of the upper branches are shown. The left branch has already melted out in this photo, taken on May 31.

COLORADO SNOW CLIMBS

15. Flattop Mountain— Dragons Tail Couloir

ELEVATION GAIN	2,540 feet
ROUND-TRIP DISTANCE	5.8 miles
STARTING ELEVATION	9,462 feet
HIGHEST ELEVATION	11,800 feet
BEST MONTHS TO CLIMB	May and early June
DIFFICULTY	A steep snow climb with the possibility of some mixed climbing (M2-3)
GEAR	A rope, crampons, ice tools, helmet
MAP	McHenrys Peak 7.5 minute

GETTING THERE: From the major intersection of U.S. 34 and 36 in the town of Estes Park, drive west through town on U.S. 36. Turn south in 0.4 mile and continue on U.S. 36 as it turns west toward Rocky Mountain National Park. Turn left (south) on Bear Lake Road after 4.4 miles, and drive to its terminus at the large parking area after 14 miles.

Consider using the shuttle bus rather than driving to Bear Lake. For more information, go to: *http://www.nps.gov/romo/visit/shuttle.html.*

COMMENT: The Dragons Tail Couloir, on the south face of Flattop Mountain in Rocky Mountain National Park, is a fine example of a couloir that reliably comes into climbing shape relatively early in the spring season. The couloir offers several options depending on how late in the season you attempt a climb. The left branch is often favored early in the season, since the right-hand branch can be guarded by a significant cornice that can bar exit. In this left branch, a short, technical rock section will usually be encountered (M2-3) that may require mixed climbing techniques and possibly a rope. As the season progresses into June, the left branch will melt out completely and the right branch will become a better option. This right branch can also require climbing a short section of technical rock.

APPROACH: From the Bear Lake Parking Area, follow the trail initially south, signed to Dream Lake and Emerald Lake. The trail is normally well tracked to Emerald Lake, 1.5 miles from the trailhead. Skirt around the left (south) side of Emerald Lake to its west end. You will now be directly below the couloir, which rises to the northwest from the lake and immediately to the right of an impressive rock spire known as the Dragons Tail. Study the

couloir as you approach the lake. You should be able to see both of the upper branches of the couloir. If the left branch is in shape, all but a short, 15-foot section should be snow-covered. Also check the cornice at the top of the right branch. Based on conditions, choose one of these options.

THE CLIMB: Find a good spot near the base of the climb to don crampons and helmet, and head up talus and initially easy snow slopes that steepen to approximately 45 degrees as you reach the fork in the couloir. Based on the conditions you observed earlier, choose your route. If the left branch is in shape, expect steep snow with a 15-foot easy, mixed section to negotiate. On May 31, 2006, this left branch had already melted out, so I chose to head to the right. A 20-foot section of wet rock required a bit of easy, mixed climbing (M2) to gain the upper part of the gully. From here, steep snow led to the cornice, which could be bypassed on either side. I chose a 60-degree snow slope (best climbed with two ice tools)

Approaching the crux of the left branch in good conditions.   PHOTO BY KEVIN CRAIG

on the left that crossed over to the head of the left branch and an easy exit.

DESCENT: The climb tops out on the broad east ridge of Flattop Mountain. To descend, head northwest to intersect the Flattop Mountain Trail. Follow the trail back down to the Bear Lake Parking Area. Note that the trail can be difficult to follow as it reaches treeline, so pay careful attention.

This snow ramp to the left of the cornice provides a very nice exit option to avoid the cornice that guards the right branch.

SEE MAP PAGE 231

Sunrise on the south face of Torreys Peak. The Dead Dog couloir is the obvious line that reaches the ridge just right of the summit.

PHOTO BY DAVE COOPER

COLORADO SNOW CLIMBS

16. Torreys Peak—Dead Dog Couloir

ELEVATION GAIN	3,100 feet
ROUND-TRIP DISTANCE	6.5 miles
STARTING ELEVATION	11,250 feet at the summer trailhead
HIGHEST ELEVATION	14,267 feet
BEST MONTHS TO CLIMB	Late May or June; by the end of June, the snow is often gone and the couloir becomes an ugly and dangerous scree slope
DIFFICULTY	Steep snow
GEAR	Crampons, ice ax, snowshoes, and helmet
MAP	Grays Peak 7.5 minute

GETTING THERE: Drive to the Bakerville exit on Interstate 70, 4.3 miles west of Silver Plume. Head south on the rough road up Stevens Gulch for 3 miles to the summer trailhead, just beyond the forest service boundary. Early in the season it may not be possible to drive all the way to the summer trailhead, so be prepared for a longer approach.

COMMENT: This climb is an old favorite and one that I've done with friends on many occasions. It is popular as a training climb for those heading off on spring and summer expeditions to places such as South America. Catch this climb early enough in the morning for the snow to still be frozen, and keep an eye open for rockfall when the sun hits the top of the route.

APPROACH: If you're parked lower down the road, continue up the Stevens Gulch road to the summer trailhead. From here, immediately cross the footbridge and follow the Grays Peak Trail as it heads southwest up the valley, past the southeast slopes of Kelso Mountain. Usually there is a packed trail to follow, hopefully avoiding the willows! Since you should be hiking this section of trail before dawn, the snow is probably still frozen, allowing the snowshoes to stay on your pack. This is unlikely to be the case on your return. Two miles beyond the summer trailhead, it is time to leave the trail and head into the basin directly below the east face of Torreys Peak. The Dead Dog Couloir is the prominent couloir that heads up near the middle of the face, topping out approximately 100 feet to the right of the summit.

THE CLIMB: After donning crampons and getting out your ice ax and helmet, head up the gradually steepening snow slope. The couloir steepens

One of the local residents.

and narrows, reaching approximately 50 degrees near the top after 1,500 feet of climbing. The couloir exits onto the Kelso Ridge immediately to the left of a gray rock tower, normally the crux of the Kelso Ridge Route on Torreys. After you gain the ridge, it is a short scramble up snow and scree to the summit of Torreys Peak.

DESCENT: To descend, follow the trail down the southeast ridge to the Torreys-Grays saddle at 13,700 feet. Continue southeast until you have cleared the large cornice that forms every year. Traverse on snow or, if visible, the trail, to rejoin the Grays Peak Trail. Continue down the well-marked trail back to your vehicle. Keep an eye out for some of the year-round residents of the area—mountain goats and ptarmigan.

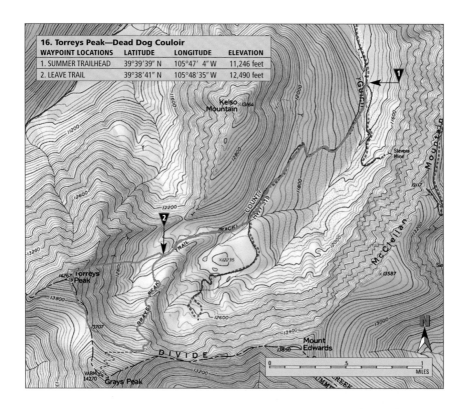

16. Torreys Peak—Dead Dog Couloir			
WAYPOINT LOCATIONS	LATITUDE	LONGITUDE	ELEVATION
1. SUMMER TRAILHEAD	39°39′39″ N	105°47′ 4″ W	11,246 feet
2. LEAVE TRAIL	39°38′41″ N	105°48′35″ W	12,490 feet

Climbing steep snow high on Dead Dog.

PHOTO BY DAVE COOPER

Climbers topping out on Skywalker. This direct exit is quite steep, approaching 60 degrees, and very enjoyable in these conditions.

17. South Arapaho Peak— South Couloir (Skywalker)

ELEVATION GAIN	3,280 feet
ROUND-TRIP DISTANCE	6.0 miles
STARTING ELEVATION	10,172 feet
HIGHEST ELEVATION	3,397 feet
BEST MONTHS TO CLIMB	Mid to late May through June; once the direct exit has melted out, this climb is less fun
DIFFICULTY	Very steep snow
GEAR	Crampons, ice ax and a second tool, snowshoes, and helmet; some climbers may want to use a rope and protect the direct exit with pickets
MAPS	Monarch Lake 7.5 minute East Portal 7.5 minute

GETTING THERE: From Nederland (west of Boulder on U.S. 119), drive west on U.S. 119 to the Eldora junction at the edge of town. Turn right here and head west, staying straight after 1.4 miles, where the road to the Eldora Ski Area takes off to the left. At 4.0 miles, the road turns to dirt (shortly after passing through the town of Eldora). Continue to the Buckingham Campground (shown on the map as the Fourth of July Campground) at 8.8 miles. Trailhead parking is just uphill from the campground.

COMMENT: This is simply one of the best couloir climbs in Colorado. Combining great location and interesting climbing, this is a "must do." Enjoy 1,800 feet of snow.

While I have climbed this route in early May before the road was open to the Fourth of July Campground, that adds 7 or 8 miles to the round-trip distance and makes for an extremely long day. The road is usually open around the middle of May. It is also better to wait for the surface layer of snow to slough off and for any cornice remnants to fall before attempting this couloir. One of the reasons why the snow conditions in the couloir can be so good is that, although the couloir faces south, all but the exit is inset such that the snow is shielded from early-morning sun. This produces excellent cramponing conditions.

Steep climbing on great snow.

PHOTO BY DAVE COOPER

APPROACH: Follow the Arapaho Pass Trail from the trailhead to the vicinity of the Fourth of July Mine, approximately 1.7 miles from the trailhead. Traverse on snow to the base of the couloir.

THE CLIMB: Start out on moderate slopes, often cluttered with large piles of old avalanche debris. The grade gradually steepens as the couloir narrows. The average grade is around 34 degrees, but at the exit, the grade can reach 60 degrees. Many people will want a second ice tool and possibly a belay for this steepness, especially if the snow is still firm. The views in the upper part of the route are spectacular as the grade steepens and the walls close in around you. The steepest part of the exit can sometimes be avoided on the right, where a moat may form around the rock. If the direct exit has melted out, it is possible to exit left via one of two snow fingers a little below. These usually deposit you on nasty scree slopes and have little to recommend them, so use them only as a bailout. From the top of the couloir, the summit of South Arapaho Peak, complete with a bronze plaque identifying the surrounding features, is a short distance to the east.

DESCENT: Follow the southeast ridge toward the saddle with Unnamed Point 13,038. Earlier in the season, it is possible to plunge-step down moderate snowfields before reaching the saddle, returning to the base of the climb where you may have stashed snowshoes, etc. Don't head down too soon or you'll find yourself on tedious and possibly dangerous slopes. Later in the season, when the Arapaho Glacier Trail is visible, use this trail as much as possible to avoid damaging the fragile tundra.

Skywalker, seen from the Diamond Lake Trail.

PHOTO BY DAVE COOPER

SEE MAP PAGE 125

Approaching Upper Diamond Lake. The Snow Lion takes the direct line to the summit of Mount Jasper. The broad snowfield descending from the left ridge is Gatorade.

18. Mount Jasper Snow Climbs (Featuring the Snow Lion)

ELEVATION GAIN	3,400 feet
ROUND-TRIP DISTANCE	9.0 miles
STARTING ELEVATION	10,172 feet
HIGHEST ELEVATION	12,923 feet
BEST MONTHS TO CLIMB	Mid May through June
DIFFICULTY	Steep snow
GEAR	Crampons, ice ax and possibly second ice tool, snowshoes, and helmet
MAPS	Monarch Lake 7.5 minute East Portal 7.5 minute

GETTING THERE: From Nederland (west of Boulder on U.S. 119), drive west on U.S. 119 to the Eldora junction at the edge of town. Turn right here and head west, staying straight after 1.4 miles, where the road to the Eldora Ski Area takes off to the left. At 4.0 miles, the road turns to dirt (shortly after passing through the town of Eldora). Continue to the Buckingham Campground (shown on the map as the Fourth of July Campground) at 8.8 miles. Trailhead parking is just uphill from the campground.

COMMENT: Mount Jasper is one of the gems of the Indian Peaks Wilderness. Its remote setting and outstanding snow lines make this mountain a personal favorite. It takes a bit of an effort to get to the southeast face of Jasper, especially early in the season, but once you are there, I think you'll agree it is worth it. Great views and great climbing await you. The direct line on the southeast face, which deposits you within a few feet of the summit, is known to climbers as the Snow Lion. This line offers several variations, depending on the season. On May 18, 2007, remnants of a cornice blocked the direct exit, but a beautiful, steep snow rib allowed the cornice to be passed on the right. Because the face receives sun from early morning, an early start is essential to avoid a wallow and possibly worse.

APPROACH: From the Fourth of July Campground, take the Arapaho Pass Trail for 1.1 miles to the signed junction with the Diamond Lake Trail. Follow the Diamond Lake Trail for approximately 1.4 miles. This sounds simple, but in May the trail is difficult to follow precisely. You will need map and compass skills (and possibly a GPS) to navigate your way. The bridge

Topping out on Jasper's summit. PHOTO BY RANDY MURPHY

crossing the North Fork of Middle Boulder Creek becomes important to find when the snow bridges across the creek become unsafe due to the significant flow in the spring. Also note that the Diamond Lake Trail has been rerouted in part and is not as shown on the 1976 map.

From Diamond Lake, head northwest up the drainage to Upper Diamond Lake and pick your line.

THE CLIMB: Head up the obvious line in the center of the face. If conditions deteriorate, a lower-angle option is available to the right. Or, with stable snow, try the left branch that heads up to Jasper's south ridge. This latter option, known as the Snow Leopard, comes into shape later in the season after the cornice has gone.

Assuming you stay on the Snow Lion Route, you will encounter a rock band perhaps 50 feet below the top of the couloir. The snow around this rock band is the first to melt out and requires care to avoid some large holes that may be hidden under rotten snow. Negotiate this area and choose an exit line. As mentioned above, cornice remnants on the left side may force you onto a snow rib on the right. This rib provides an airy position and a fitting finish to the climb. The average slope on Snow Lion is 39 degrees, but the finish approaches 50 degrees.

The cornices guarding the Snow Leopard.
PHOTO BY DAVE COOPER

DESCENT: From the summit, walk south then southeast down the ridge to the top of a large, relatively low-angle snowfield known as Gatorade. The lower edge of this snowfield is no steeper than 34 degrees and makes a good glissade. Note that Gatorade is a fine practice slope and can be used to ascend Jasper, especially later in the season when the other routes have melted out. I've used this snowfield in the past to teach snow-climbing techniques to mountaineering students.

SEE MAP PAGE 125

Topping out on Juliet. Some of the other fine lines can be seen behind the climber.

19. Mount Neva—
Northeast Cirque (Featuring Juliet)

ELEVATION GAIN	2,700 feet
ROUND-TRIP DISTANCE	8.2 miles if descending the northeast slopes or 9.1 miles if descending via the North Fork drainage
STARTING ELEVATION	10,172 feet
HIGHEST ELEVATION	12,814 feet
BEST MONTHS TO CLIMB	Mid May through June
DIFFICULTY	Moderate snow
GEAR	Crampons, ice ax, snowshoes, and helmet
MAPS	Monarch Lake 7.5 minute East Portal 7.5 minute

GETTING THERE: From Nederland (west of Boulder on U.S. 119), drive west on U.S. 119 to the Eldora junction at the edge of town. Turn right here and head west, staying straight after 1.4 miles, where the road to the Eldora Ski Area takes off to the left. At 4.0 miles, the road turns to dirt (shortly after passing through the town of Eldora). Continue to the Buckingham Campground (shown on the map as the Fourth of July Campground) at 8.8 miles. Trailhead parking is just uphill from the campground.

COMMENT: Neva's northeast cirque is home to several, mainly short, moderate snow climbs. This might be a good spot for those who are just getting into snow climbing, although choosing a descent route (as always) requires skill and good judgment. While Juliet is usually the first line to come into shape in the spring, several more excellent lines exist that are all steeper. Immediately to the right of Juliet is a corniced line called Desdemona. Save this for later in the season when the cornice has calved off. Also, check out several other lines above this bowl, facing more directly east. You will probably end up making several pilgrimages to this cirque to sample all that it has to offer. Because the cirque receives early-morning sun, get there extra early to avoid wallowing in soft snow.

APPROACH: From the trailhead at the Fourth of July Campground, head up the Arapaho Pass Trail for 3 miles to Arapaho Pass. Take the left-hand fork on the Caribou Pass Trail to Lake Dorothy. Circle around the southeast side of the lake, and contour into the large cirque below the northeast face of Mount Neva—a stunning place.

THE CLIMB: Once you are in the cirque, there will be several enticing options for a climb. Conditions and the time of year will dictate the best line. Cornices threaten several lines early in the season, so pick carefully. A good choice early in the season is Juliet, a shallow couloir that tops out on Neva's northwest ridge 100 yards from the summit. This is to the left of the obvious, heavily corniced line. The nondescript northeast slopes to the left of the climb offer the preferred descent. Juliet provides 400 feet of vertical with an average steepness of 40 degrees. Rock outcrops narrow the couloir in its midsection, which is also the steepest part of the climb. From the ridge, it is a short walk left to the summit of Neva.

DESCENT: Several descent lines are possible. Either down climb the route, pick a line down the northeast slopes to the south of the climb, or continue south over the summit of Neva for a quarter mile to a shallow gully that descends directly to the lakes immediately south of Neva's summit. From there, work your way back down the North Fork drainage and rejoin the Arapaho Pass Trail.

Approaching the narrow section of the climb.
PHOTO BY DAVE COOPER

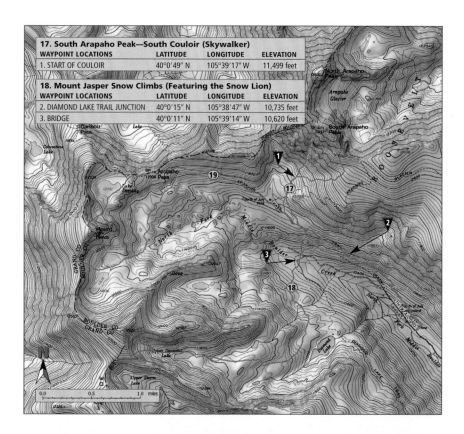

17. South Arapaho Peak—South Couloir (Skywalker)			
WAYPOINT LOCATIONS	LATITUDE	LONGITUDE	ELEVATION
1. START OF COULOIR	40°0′49″ N	105°39′17″ W	11,499 feet

18. Mount Jasper Snow Climbs (Featuring the Snow Lion)			
WAYPOINT LOCATIONS	LATITUDE	LONGITUDE	ELEVATION
2. DIAMOND LAKE TRAIL JUNCTION	40°0′15″ N	105°38′47″ W	10,735 feet
3. BRIDGE	40°0′11″ N	105°39′14″ W	10,620 feet

Neva's northeast cirque. Juliet is left of center in this photo, with the obvious hourglass shape. The northeast slopes used for the descent are farther left. PHOTO BY DAVE COOPER

The Savage Couloir, seen from the east ridge. This striking line offers continuously
interesting climbing with several exit possibilities.

COLORADO SNOW CLIMBS

20. Savage Mountain— The Savage Couloir

TOTAL ELEVATION	3,280 feet
ROUND-TRIP DISTANCE	7.5 miles
STARTING ELEVATION	10,020 feet
HIGHEST ELEVATION	13,139 feet
BEST MONTH TO CLIMB	Late May through July; the snow stays well into the summer, although when the top section melts out, it reveals some ugly scree
DIFFICULTY	Steep snow
GEAR	Crampons, ice ax and a second tool, snowshoes, and helmet
MAPS	Mount of the Holy Cross 7.5 minute Mount Jackson 7.5 minute

GETTING THERE: Take the Minturn exit (exit 171) from Interstate 70 and drive south on U.S. 24 for 12.9 miles to Homestake Road. Take this washboard road (recently graded, though) for 7.9 miles to a road junction signed to Missouri Creek and Holy Cross City, 1.0 mile past Gold Park Campground. Turn right at this junction onto Forest Service Road 704, and drive 2.2 miles to a T- junction at the Fancy Lake and adjacent Missouri Lakes trailheads. The last couple of miles are rougher, but they are usually passable by most passenger cars.

COMMENT: Several years ago, Kevin Craig had noticed a striking snow line on a nearby peak while on the summit of Mount of the Holy Cross. He later identified the mountain as Savage Mountain, also in the Holy Cross Wilderness. I had seen the gully on a summer hike to the area and could see the potential, so we decided to check it out. What a good eye Kevin had. The climb is deeply inset into the northeast face of Savage and offers well over a thousand feet of snow climbing.

APPROACH: From the Missouri Lakes Trailhead, follow the trail for approximately 2 miles until you reach a relatively flat area near 10,970 feet. The exact location to leave the trail will depend on the season; earlier and you may be able to cross the streams on snow bridges, but later and you may have to be creative. We were able to find a crossing on iced-up logs by donning crampons. Make a rising traverse southwest around Savage's

Climbing the lower slopes
of the couloir.
PHOTO BY DAVE COOPER

southeast ridge, aiming for the cirque directly south of the lake at 11,380 feet. A flat area at the base of the couloir makes a good place to prepare for the climb.

THE CLIMB: The angle is quite constant, averaging around 40 degrees, with occasional steeper sections that may locally reach 50 degrees. It is best to stay a little to the left of the runnel that forms in the middle of the couloir, because this is where any rockfall tends to be funneled. Since the route sees early-morning sun, be alert for any rocks that are dislodged spontaneously, mainly from the right-hand wall.

There are several intriguing exit variations. The direct exit is quite aesthetic as long as it holds the snow, while exits to the left may be good if they are not guarded by cornices. Assuming you take the direct exit, you will emerge on the summit ridge only a short distance from the summit. The views of the Holy Cross Wilderness are stunning and may inspire you with several other potential snow climbs in the area.

DESCENT: How to descend? At the beginning of June, there was still enough snow in the trees to make the descent a challenge. Descending the northeast ridge is the best option, then cutting left across a saddle at 11,700 feet and heading back to your ascent track. Several variations on this are possible. The bowl between the northeast ridge and the east ridge can provide some of the best boot-skiing we've found in Colorado. Therefore, a reasonable option is to head down into this bowl, then traverse back to the 11,700-foot saddle on the northeast ridge. Continuing down lower into the previously mentioned bowl almost guarantees a miserable wallow in the trees and is not recommended.

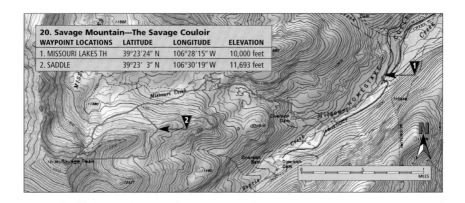

20. Savage Mountain—The Savage Couloir			
WAYPOINT LOCATIONS	**LATITUDE**	**LONGITUDE**	**ELEVATION**
1. MISSOURI LAKES TH	39°23′24″ N	106°28′15″ W	10,000 feet
2. SADDLE	39°23′ 3″ N	106°30′19″ W	11,693 feet

Approaching the top, several possible exits become apparent.

PHOTO BY DAVE COOPER

The north face of Democrat. The inset north couloir can be seen at the extreme right of photo. Other enticing lines are obvious, but they melt out earlier.

COLORADO SNOW CLIMBS

21. Mount Democrat—North Couloir

ELEVATION GAIN	2,600 feet
ROUND-TRIP DISTANCE	9.9 miles
STARTING ELEVATION	10,900 feet
HIGHEST ELEVATION	13,600 feet
BEST MONTHS TO CLIMB	June through July
DIFFICULTY	Moderate snow
GEAR	Ice ax, crampons (depending on season), and helmet
MAPS	Alma 7.5 minute Climax 7.5 minute Copper Mountain 7.5 minute

GETTING THERE: One mile south of Hoosier Pass on Colorado 9, take the sharp exit west onto Park County Road 4. Follow County Road 4 downhill, staying straight on County Road 4 after 0.8 mile, where Nuthatch Drive makes a sharp turn to the left. Two-tenths mile after this junction there is a three-way junction. County Road 4 turns sharply left and the middle fork continues slightly downhill to the Montgomery Reservoir Dam. Take the right fork (Forest Service Road 408), which passes through an open gate and contours above the reservoir to a parking area by the spillway, a total of 1.6 miles from Colorado 9. Later in the spring, the gate will be open, and it is possible to park approximately one-third mile further. A little before the Magnolia Mill the road becomes very rough.

COMMENT: As mentioned in the Wheeler Peak description, the upper basin of the Middle Fork of the South Platte River tends to hold snow longer than surrounding areas. Perhaps the finest pure snow climb in this valley is on the north face of Mount Democrat. In a deeply inset couloir, this moderate route has wonderful position and a sense of remoteness that I never tire of.

The climb's moderate angle and scenic location make this an excellent introduction to couloir climbing. Once you have experienced how much fun you can have in the alpine environment, you'll be hooked.

Note: The normal finish to this climb involves scrambling up Democrat's north ridge to the summit, then descending to the Cameron saddle and taking the climbers' trail back down into Platte Gulch. At the time of writing, this route to the summit of Democrat is closed to public access, so that option no longer exists; (I hope that situation will change at some point).

Topping out onto the north ridge.

PHOTO BY DAVE COOPER

APPROACH: From the parking area, head southwest on the road as it contours around to the west end of the lake, through a closed gate. The road heads up the valley, passing under the Magnolia Mill.

After passing the mill, the jeep trail stays to the right of the drainage to avoid private property, paralleling the river. After 2.9 miles, the road starts to diagonal up the right-hand side of the valley toward the lake. Look for a fainter road taking off to the left, partway up the hillside. This road to the left is reached shortly after crossing the stream that flows across the road. Follow this lower road as it contours into the basin below Democrat's north face. You'll start to get glimpses of the couloir at the extreme right edge of the face. When the road peters out, continue to traverse southwest into Upper Platte Gulch, and head for the flat section at the base of the climb.

THE CLIMB: Just head up the snow and enjoy this moderate classic that averages close to 35 degrees as it gains 700 feet. In the steepest sections the angle can reach 45 degrees. The exit onto the ridge provides breathtaking views.

DESCENT: Due to the closure of Democrat's summit, it is necessary to either descend the couloir or down climb the lower north ridge (expect a short section of Class 4 terrain) to the ridge point at 13,460 feet, where a northeast-trending spur allows you to exit back down to the basin and eventually the jeep road.

Starting up the couloir.

SEE MAP PAGE 97

The north face of Meeker, split by the Flying Buttress. Dreamweaver follows the ribbon of snow immediately left of the buttress.

22. Mount Meeker—Dreamweaver

ELEVATION GAIN	4,700 feet, of which approximately 1,000 feet are gained on the climb itself
ROUND-TRIP DISTANCE	10.1 miles
STARTING ELEVATION	9,450 feet
HIGHEST ELEVATION	13,911 feet
BEST MONTHS TO CLIMB	May and June
DIFFICULTY	A long trail approach to a technical mixed snow, ice, and rock climb; conditions vary, but typically expect 5.4, AI3, and steep snow
GEAR	Conditions vary widely, so be prepared for anything; cruxes are usually quite short, so unless you expect to rope up for the entire climb, a 30-meter rope will usually be sufficient; a couple of ice screws and a light alpine rock rack for protection; a helmet; two ice tools and crampons
MAPS	Longs Peak 7.5 minute Allens Park 7.5 minute

GETTING THERE: Drive north from Lyons on Colorado 7 from its junction with U.S. 36 for 25.1 miles or go south on Colorado 7 from its intersection with U.S. 36 in Estes Park. Turn west at the sign for Longs Peak Area and drive 1.1 miles to park at the Longs Peak Ranger Station. Rocky Mountain National Park fees are not collected at this location.

COMMENT: One of the finest moderate alpine routes in Rocky Mountain National Park, Dreamweaver offers the aspiring alpinist a chance to test his or her mettle. Depending on conditions, it may be a simple steep snow climb, a nice mixed route (snow, ice, and rock), or, on occasion in the autumn, a fine sustained ice climb. The route typically comes into shape sometime in May, but conditions continuously change as the snow melts, revealing more rock. When nighttime temperatures fall below freezing, ice flows are created. By late spring and early summer, much of the snow and ice has melted, leaving more difficult rock climbing in the 5.4 to 5.6 range. When this climb is in shape, there can be several parties heading up to climb it, so get an early start to avoid the hazards of being behind another party.

APPROACH: From the Longs Peak Trailhead, follow the Longs Peak Trail for 3.1 miles to the saddle on Mills Moraine, where the Chasm Lake Trail

Climbers approaching Dreamweaver.

PHOTO BY DAVE COOPER

divides from the Longs Peak Trail. A variation on this approach is described in the Longs Peak–North Face (Climb 8) route description. The solar outhouse located on Mills Moraine makes this a natural spot for a rest stop. Continue on the trail toward Chasm Lake and cross a snow slope above Peacock Pool, which is often icy in the early morning. Upon reaching the ranger hut below Chasm Lake, leave the trail and head south toward the Flying Buttress, a dominant feature on Mount Meeker's north face. Dreamweaver is immediately to the left (east) of the Flying Buttress.

THE CLIMB: Start up the moderate snowfield and reach the point where the gully narrows to a few feet in width. The first crux may be located in this first narrow section. Continue up on easier ground to a point near the top of the Flying Buttress. From the relatively flat spot near the top of the Flying Buttress, the gully bears left, but there are several different variations, all reasonable, that you can use to get into the upper part of the route in about 30 feet. There are likely to be two more cruxes in this next section, the lower of these two being the more difficult.

The third and final crux can be the sweetest of the day—30 feet of good water ice (WI3).

Climbing up over this last challenge deposits you on the summit snowfield. From here it is a simple scramble on snow and talus to the summit ridge. Turn right and enjoy a short scramble on good rock to Mount Meeker's tiny summit.

DESCENT: To descend, continue west from the Meeker summit and pick up a trail leading down to the Loft, the giant flat area between Meeker and Longs. This trail can be tricky to follow when it is partially covered by snow, but the general direction should be obvious. From the Loft, look for a series of large rock cairns leading down to a ramp on the east margin of the Loft. This route avoids the head wall immediately below the Loft. Carefully take the ramp as it cuts back to the left and deposits you on the moderate snow slope below the Loft. Be aware that this slope can avalanche. Make sure that you're here early enough in the day. A quick glissade and some talus-hopping get you back to the ranger hut and the Chasm Lake Trail. From here, heading back to the car is nothing more than a long trudge down the trail.

One of the mixed steps to be negotiated.
PHOTO BY DAVE COOPER

A windy day at the base of the route.

Sunrise over the Twin Sisters.

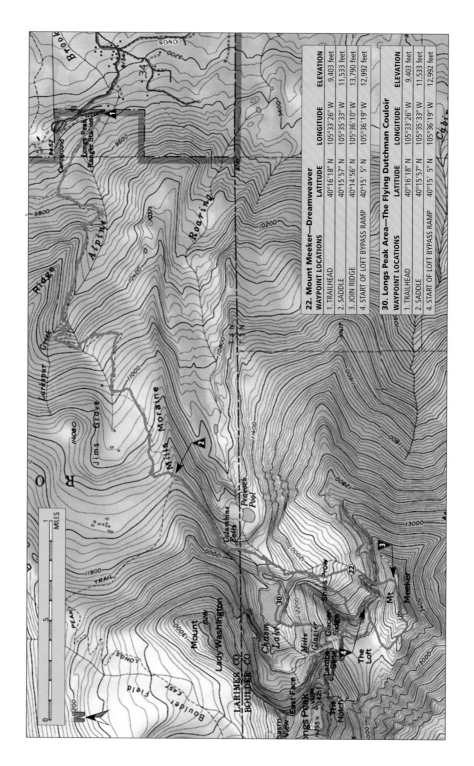

22. Mount Meeker—Dreamweaver

WAYPOINT LOCATIONS	LATITUDE	LONGITUDE	ELEVATION
1. TRAILHEAD	40°16'18" N	105°33'26" W	9,403 feet
2. SADDLE	40°15'57" N	105°35'33" W	11,533 feet
3. JOIN RIDGE	40°14'56" N	105°36'10" W	13,790 feet
4. START OF LOFT BYPASS RAMP	40°15' 5" N	105°36'19" W	12,992 feet

30. Longs Peak Area—The Flying Dutchman Couloir

WAYPOINT LOCATIONS	LATITUDE	LONGITUDE	ELEVATION
1. TRAILHEAD	40°16'18" N	105°33'26" W	9,403 feet
2. SADDLE	40°15'57" N	105°35'33" W	11,533 feet
4. START OF LOFT BYPASS RAMP	40°15' 5" N	105°36'19" W	12,992 feet

The east face of Fletcher Mountain, showing the two routes described. The left couloir provides a dramatic exit onto the southeast ridge route. PHOTO BY DAVE COOPER

COLORADO SNOW CLIMBS

23. Fletcher Mountain— East Face Routes

ELEVATION GAIN	2,900 feet from the McCullough Gulch Trailhead
ROUND-TRIP DISTANCE	3.7 miles up and 4.0 miles down to the Monte Cristo Trailhead; an additional 2.5 miles back to the McCullough Gulch Trailhead (it may be worth arranging a car shuttle, leaving a vehicle at either end)
STARTING ELEVATION	10,920 feet
HIGHEST ELEVATION	13,951 feet
BEST MONTHS TO CLIMB	Late May through June
DIFFICULTY	Very steep snow
GEAR	Crampons, ice ax and a second tool, snowshoes, and helmet; most climbers will want to use a rope if planning to climb the left-hand variation, protecting the exit using pickets or rock gear
MAPS	Copper Mountain 7.5 minute Breckenridge 7.5 minute

GETTING THERE: From Colorado 9, 2.4 miles north of Hoosier Pass, turn west onto Blue Lakes Road. After 0.1 mile, turn right (northeast) and follow this road for 2.1 miles to the McCullough Gulch Trailhead. In early season, this road is probably snow covered and not drivable. On May 21, 2007, it was possible to drive a little way past the summer trailhead.

COMMENT: The East Face of Fletcher Mountain may offer the most impressive aspect of any on this rugged peak. Flanked on the right by the Rockfountain Ridge and on the left by the mass of Quandary Peak, the views of this face as you approach the head of McCullough Gulch are breathtaking. Splitting the face are two prominent couloirs. The direct line takes the right couloir through a narrow rock constriction and then doglegs left to hit the southeast ridge almost at the summit. The left variation is the steeper of the two and reaches the southeast ridge a little lower down. In early-season conditions, the direct (right-hand) variation is likely to be your best bet, since the left-hand variation may be guarded by a cornice. Once the snow at the constriction on the right-hand route has melted out (mid June), the left-hand couloir beckons.

APPROACH: From the McCullough Gulch Trailhead, follow the road as it

Steep climbing for the final fifty feet.

PHOTO BY KEVIN CRAIG

turns left immediately past the gate closure and heads uphill. When you are 0.4 mile beyond the gate, you'll pass some mine buildings on your left. The signs here leave you in no doubt that you should stay away from the buildings. Continue on the trail, passing the unnamed lake on its north side at 11,920 feet. Stop and take a look at Quandary Peak's north couloir, directly across the lake from you. Occasional cairns lead the way from here as you head further up the drainage in the direction of Atlantic Peak. Eventually, the drainage curves to the southwest, paralleling the Rockfountain Ridge (the ridge connecting Atlantic Peak with Fletcher). Make your way to the unnamed lake at 12,766 feet, directly under Fletcher's East Face.

THE CLIMB: From the lake, you have several options to reach the upper face. The rock rib to the left (south) of the lake provides a reasonable approach path, depositing you in front of the couloirs at 13,400 feet. If snow conditions permit, you may choose to climb the snow slope directly from the lake. Choose your line and have fun. As mentioned above, the right-hand variation is the gentler of the two, averaging 42 degrees, while the left-hand variation can provide a steeper climb, becoming almost vertical near the top. You may want a rope for this one.

DESCENT: The safest route down is to follow the southeast ridge route down to Blue Lakes Reservoir, then continue back to your vehicle. This can be a long day. When the cornices have fallen down, it may be possible to descend the southeast ridge to the Quandary–Fletcher saddle and drop back into McCullough Gulch.

Belaying the exit.

PHOTO BY GINNI GREER

SEE MAP PAGE 89

The northeast couloir, shown in the upper center of the photo, tops out at the saddle between the two summits of the "Citadel"

PHOTO BY DAVE COOPER

24. "Citadel Peak" Couloirs

ELEVATION GAIN	2,950 feet
ROUND-TRIP DISTANCE	7.6 miles
STARTING ELEVATION	10,296 feet
HIGHEST ELEVATION	13,294 feet
BEST MONTHS TO CLIMB	Mid May to mid July; by the end of July, the snow is melted out of the northeast couloir
DIFFICULTY	Moderate snow
GEAR	Crampons, ice ax, snowshoes (in early season), and helmet
MAPS	Loveland Pass 7.5 minute Grays Peak 7.5 minute

GETTING THERE: Take exit 218 from Interstate 70, 2.8 miles west of the Bakerville exit. Park in the large parking area on the north side of the highway. The trailhead is located near the bathroom.

COMMENT: The "Citadel's" rugged aspect at the head of Herman Gulch and Dry Gulch catches the eye from several locations. One of the best views of the peak is from the vicinity of Loveland Pass. From spring into summer, the northeast couloir offers a moderate snow climb to the saddle between the north and south summits. The normal route to climb the "Citadel" uses the southwest couloir to reach the same saddle and offers an alternate, shorter snow climb, as well as a descent route.

APPROACH: From the parking area, take the Herman Gulch Trail up to the basin below the east face of the peak. In May, the trail will still be snowed in and skis or snowshoes will be necessary, if not for the hike in then certainly for the walk out. The northeast couloir should become obvious as the drainage curves toward the west. This couloir ascends below the "Citadel"-Pettingell ridge to the right of the south summit. Head up the slopes to the base of the climb and prepare for an enjoyable ascent.

THE CLIMB: Once you are in the couloir, the slope averages around 40 degrees and is relatively constant. The upper section of the climb is shaded by the mass of the south summit in the early morning hours and could be icy, so you may be happy to have the crampons on. The route tops out on a wind-sculpted saddle. From here it is a simple Class 3 scramble to the higher, north summit.

At the saddle. The summit is to the left.

DESCENT: Return to the saddle and down climb the short but steep gully to the southwest. As soon as possible, start traversing southeast around the base of the south summit until you can gain the "Citadel"-Bethel ridge where the ridge becomes broad. The slopes on this traverse are subject to sliding early in the season, so care is necessary. Remember that it is always possible to set anchors in the rock and belay or simul-climb across this slope if it is suspect. Walk down the ridge until you find a suitable spot to head back down into the basin. Under the right conditions, this can be a nice glissade. Rejoin your ascent track and head back to the parking area.

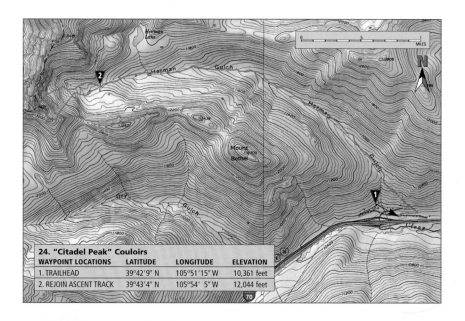

| 24. "Citadel Peak" Couloirs | | | |
WAYPOINT LOCATIONS	LATITUDE	LONGITUDE	ELEVATION
1. TRAILHEAD	39°42'9" N	105°51'15" W	10,361 feet
2. REJOIN ASCENT TRACK	39°43'4" N	105°54' 5" W	12,044 feet

Descend the southwest gully to reach the "Citadel"-Bethel connecting ridge.

The complex east ridge of "East Thorn". The bottom of the couloir used to gain the ridge is just visible on the far right in this photo.

PHOTO BY DAVE COOPER

25. "East Thorn"—North Couloir

ELEVATION GAIN	5,330 feet from Mesa Cortina Trailhead; 4,640 feet from Willowbrook Trailhead
ROUND-TRIP DISTANCE	18.3 miles from Mesa Cortina Trailhead; 12 miles from Willowbrook Trailhead
STARTING ELEVATION	Mesa Cortina Trailhead, 9,250 feet; Willowbrook Trailhead, 9,000 feet
HIGHEST ELEVATION	13,333 feet
BEST MONTHS TO CLIMB	Mid-June through mid-July
DIFFICULTY	Moderate snow, Class 4 scrambling; some groups use a short length of rope for the section just before the summit
GEAR	Crampons, ice ax, helmet
MAPS	Willow Lakes 7.5 minute Dillon 7.5 minute

GETTING THERE: Two trailheads provide access to "East Thorn." If you plan on a day climb, the Willowbrook Trailhead is your best option. Since overnight parking isn't allowed there, if you are backpacking in you'll need to use the Mesa Cortina Trailhead and face the much longer approach.

Mesa Cortina Trailhead: From the Silverthorne exit (exit 205) off Interstate 70, go north and almost immediately turn left (southwest) on Wildernest Road. Go 0.2 mile to Adams Road. Turn right (north) and almost immediately make a left (west) onto Buffalo Mountain Drive. Follow Buffalo Mountain Drive for 0.8 mile to its intersection with Lakeview Drive. Turn right (north) on Lakeview Drive and drive 0.4 mile to Aspen Drive. Turn left on Aspen Drive and continue 0.1 mile to the Mesa Cortina Trailhead parking area.

Willowbrook Trailhead: From the intersection of Interstate 70 and Colorado 9 in Silverthorne, head north on Colorado 9 for 1.9 miles. Turn left (west) onto Willowbrook Road, which winds through the housing development (several speed bumps) for 1 mile to the trailhead and parking area. The trailhead is on private property, so overnight parking is not allowed.

COMMENT: Located in the heart of the Gore Range, this climb combines a moderate snow climb with an interesting Class 3 and Class 4 scramble to the summit, all in a remote and very beautiful setting. What could be better?

The view from the start of the couloir.
PHOTO BY DAVE COOPER

"East Thorn Peak" is visible from several vantage points—from Interstate 70 as you descend west from the Eisenhower Tunnel and from Colorado 9 a few miles north of Silverthorne. It is the rugged, steep peak visible just north of Red Mountain and is a poster child for the Gore Range.

APPROACH: From the Mesa Cortina Trailhead:
Hike northwest along the Mesa Cortina Trail, crossing an open meadow after 0.1 mile. After 2.6 miles, the Mesa Cortina Trail intersects the Gore Range Trail (signed, no. 60) immediately after crossing South Willow Creek. Turn right (north) onto the Gore Range Trail, and follow this historic trail as it gently undulates through the forest, crossing several drainages (including North Willow Creek at mile 4.3, where the Willowbrook Trail comes in) before reaching another signed trail junction 5.8 miles from the trailhead. Shortly before this junction you should catch a few tantalizing glimpses of your objective, "East Thorn Peak" (13,333 feet), which rises west of Salmon Lake.

Leave the Gore Range Trail here and turn left on the Willow Lakes Trail (no. 36). Note that the USGS map doesn't show this trail junction in the correct spot. After 1.6 miles on the Willow Lakes Trail you will come to another trail junction. The right fork is signed to Salmon Lake (no. 36.1A). Follow this trail and arrive at the west end of Salmon Lake in an additional 0.5 mile.

From the Willowbrook Trailhead:
This trail parallels North Willow Creek for 1.2 miles before intersecting the Gore Range Trail. From here, follow the description for the Mesa Cortina approach. This approach saves 6.4 miles round trip versus the Mesa Cortina approach.

THE CLIMB: From the west end of Salmon Lake, follow the drainage west, sometimes on a climbers' trail, until you find a good spot to cross the moraine and head toward the start of the couloir. The couloir is deeply inset, so it isn't visible until you're close to the start of it. A second snow finger (which looks quite intriguing) parallels the main couloir on its west side and can be seen earlier. Both go to the east ridge, but the main couloir exits at a deep notch in the ridge. The couloir gains a little more than 700 feet and has a remarkably constant angle of 38 degrees.

At the notch (12,740 feet), enjoy the view looking down on the Willow Lakes before turning right and heading toward the summit. The route finding is quite complex on this ridge.

Moderate snow climbing leads to the east ridge.
PHOTO BY DAVE COOPER

Follow a climbers' path as it heads up just left of the ridgeline. From the first ridge point, drop down a few feet and head for a small grassy col to the left of the ridge. From here, ledges take you back to the crest and to another false summit. Stay out of the loose gully to the left of this ridge point.

A steep down climb to a narrow catwalk puts you at the final obstacle, a small tower. To the right is an exposed climb that may require a rope, or you can do what I did—leave the pack behind and squirm up a slab on the left, under an overhang. Not elegant, but effective.

Climb back up to the crest and scramble a few feet to the true summit.

DESCENT: Reverse the route, being careful to choose the correct ridge as you head back to the notch. Descend the snow of the ascent couloir and head for the trail.

Descending the snow slopes below the couloir.

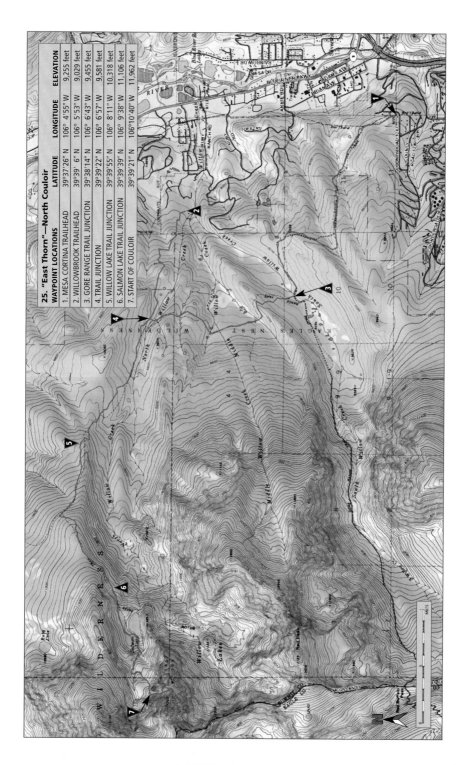

25. "East Thorn"—North Couloir			
WAYPOINT LOCATIONS	LATITUDE	LONGITUDE	ELEVATION
1. MESA CORTINA TRAILHEAD	39°37'26" N	106° 4'55" W	9,255 feet
2. WILLOWBROOK TRAILHEAD	39°39' 6" N	106° 5'53" W	9,029 feet
3. GORE RANGE TRAIL JUNCTION	39°38'14" N	106° 6'43" W	9,455 feet
4. TRAIL JUNCTION	39°39'22" N	106° 6'57" W	9,581 feet
5. WILLOW LAKE TRAIL JUNCTION	39°39'55" N	106° 8'11" W	10,318 feet
6. SALMON LAKE TRAIL JUNCTION	39°39'39" N	106° 9'38" W	11,106 feet
7. START OF COULOIR	39°39'21" N	106°10'40" W	11,962 feet

The lower section of Pacific's north couloir, seen from the east ridge. Just before reaching the cornice seen here, the climb turns sharply left for the final four hundred feet.

26. Pacific Peak—North Couloir

ELEVATION GAIN	From the water diversion dam, 2,780 feet; from the winter trailhead, add 740 feet
ROUND-TRIP DISTANCE	From the water diversion dam, 7.0 miles; from the winter trailhead, add 3.6 miles round-trip
STARTING ELEVATION	11,110 feet at the water diversion dam
HIGHEST ELEVATION	13,950 feet
BEST MONTHS TO CLIMB	Late May through early July, depending on desired conditions
DIFFICULTY	Moderate snow in early season conditions to AI3 and easy mixed climbing in early July
GEAR	Depending on the season, pickets, rock pro (a couple of knife-blade pitons may be useful), or short ice screws can be used to protect the route; rope, and helmet
MAP	Breckenridge 7.5 minute

GETTING THERE: From the Boreas Pass Road junction at the south end of Breckenridge (the last traffic light as you leave town), follow Colorado 9 for 1.7 miles south to Spruce Creek Road. Turn west onto Spruce Creek Road and follow it through a housing development to the winter trailhead parking area, 1.2 miles from Colorado 9. There is a trailhead sign here for the Mohawk Lakes Trail. After the snow melts off the road, four-wheel-drive vehicles can continue on to the water diversion dam, shortening the approach by 1.8 miles.

COMMENT: In their guidebook, *Colorado's Thirteeners, 13,800 to 13,999 Feet, From Hikes to Climbs,* Gerry and Jennifer Roach describe the North Couloir as "the finest snow climb in the Tenmile-Mosquito Range" when it is in good condition. I would add to that and say that if you are lucky enough to catch this climb at the right time, it can provide one of the best alpine ice routes anywhere in the state.

From being a moderate snow climb in May and early June, the couloir changes over the course of June into a superb and committing ice climb. Once the ice has melted out, this is no place to be, because the rock is some of the worst I've encountered.

While conditions are reliable in early season, if you're trying to catch the alpine ice conditions mentioned above, it is worth taking a few minutes to

Grabbing a bite to eat on an early season climb of the route.

preview the upper part of the route by climbing partway up the slopes leading to the Pacific-Crystal saddle. From here, you get a decent view of the upper section.

A word of caution: The northeast face of Pacific sheds lots of rock, especially in early summer. If you are climbing in this season, a super-early start is advised.

APPROACH: Follow the Mohawk Lakes Trail from the winter parking area to the Spruce Creek Road, then continue to the water diversion dam at the end of the road. Later in the season, drive to the dam. The trail takes off to the right immediately before the dam, signed to Mayflower Lake and the Mohawk Lakes. Stay left at the trail junction 0.2 mile beyond the water diversion dam, where a short detour would otherwise take you to Mayflower Lake.

Just before reaching Continental Falls, 2.5 miles from the trailhead, the trail wanders through some well-preserved log buildings. When you reach the vicinity of the falls, the trail climbs up to the left of the falls. Shortly after reaching the top of the falls, the trail passes more mine buildings.

Above the falls the terrain becomes gentler, and shortly you reach Lower Mohawk Lake and then Mohawk Lake. Continue up the valley, passing several more lakes. The highest is at an elevation of 12,447 feet. Contour around this lake and head for the bowl below the north face of Pacific. The lower part of the climb is directly above you at this point, although you cannot see the upper 400 feet. This section turns left a little below a large cornice formed on the north ridge, and heads directly to the distinctive notch just north of the summit. If conditions in the upper couloir are not to your liking, it may be possible to escape past the edge of the cornice onto the ridge.

THE CLIMB: From the basin, climb the obvious snow slope toward the large cornice on the north ridge. Shortly after passing an impressive-looking rock pinnacle on its left side, turn left into the upper part of the couloir. This section offers the steepest climbing, with brief sections that may approach 60

On July 8, the upper four hundred feet of the climb was on incredible alpine ice.

PHOTO BY DAVE COOPER

Climbers passing the prominent tower on an early season ascent.   PHOTO BY KEVIN CRAIG

degrees. The complete couloir provides 700 feet of climbing with an average angle of around 36 degrees.

Depending on conditions, climb snow or ice for 400 feet to the notch in the ridge. On July 8, 2007, I found a ribbon of superb alpine ice (AI3) that was almost continuous for 400 vertical feet, with only short, easy sections of mixed climbing on rotten rock. These are the kinds of conditions alpinists dream of. If you are climbing with a partner, be aware that you *will* knock down rock while negotiating the rock sections, so take appropriate precautions.

DESCENT: From the notch, it is a simple scramble east to the summit. From here, descend the east ridge on a trail to the plateau containing Pacific Tarn. Take one of the moderate snow slopes back into the Mohawk Lakes Basin and rejoin the trail.

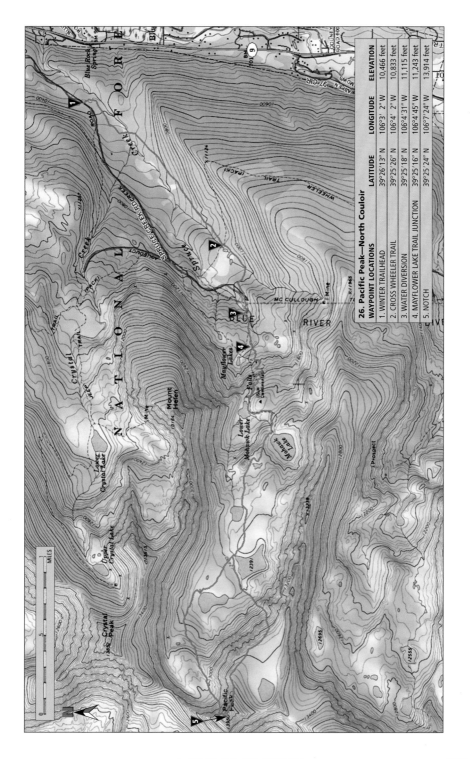

26. Pacific Peak—North Couloir			
WAYPOINT LOCATIONS	**LATITUDE**	**LONGITUDE**	**ELEVATION**
1. WINTER TRAILHEAD	39°26'13" N	106°3' 2" W	10,466 feet
2. CROSS WHEELER TRAIL	39°25'26" N	106°4' 2" W	10,833 feet
3. WATER DIVERSION	39°25'18" N	106°4'31" W	11,115 feet
4. MAYFLOWER LAKE TRAIL JUNCTION	39°25'16" N	106°4'45" W	11,243 feet
5. NOTCH	39°25'24" N	106°7'24" W	13,914 feet

The Naked Lady couloir on Snowdon Peak is visible from many locations around Molas Pass, and presents a striking form. PHOTO BY DAVE COOPER

27. Snowdon Peak—Northwest Couloir (Naked Lady Couloir)

ELEVATION GAIN	2,330 feet
ROUND-TRIP DISTANCE	6.0 miles
STARTING ELEVATION	10,750 feet
HIGHEST ELEVATION	13,077 feet
BEST MONTHS TO CLIMB	Late May through June
DIFFICULTY	Steep snow, with some moderate, mixed climbing later in the season; the descent can be challenging with snow on the ridge, with ratings from exposed Class 3 when dry to technical when wet and snow covered
GEAR	Crampons, ice ax and a second tool, snowshoes, and helmet; some climbers may want to use a rope, in which case bring a small alpine rock rack, plus a couple of knife-blade pitons, and a couple of pickets
MAP	Snowdon Peak 7.5 minute

GETTING THERE: From Silverton, take U.S. 550 south for 6.4 miles to the summit of Molas Pass. Continue south for a further 0.9 mile to the Andrews Lake Road. Turn left and follow the paved road for 0.7 mile to a parking area at Andrews Lake.

COMMENT: A few years ago, I spied this striking line while on a trip to the area and determined to go back and climb it. I had no idea at the time that it has been regularly climbed and even has a name. It was some years later that I finally had an opportunity to get on the climb. The wait was worth it. By the way, if you look at the couloir from the right angle, it looks like a person, and, with a vivid imagination, maybe female. A naked lady? You decide. With a relatively short approach and quality climbing, this is guaranteed to become a classic. What makes the climb more serious than it otherwise would be is the descent route. If you choose not to down climb the route, then the most straightforward descent is via the northeast ridge. In summer, this is rated at only Class 3, but in May the quartzite rock can be treacherous, plus unstable snow can cover up the ledges on the east side of the ridge. These ledges are the secret to keeping the route at Class 3. Experienced mountaineers will still enjoy solving the challenges of this descent; just be prepared.

APPROACH: Take the Crater Lake Trail from the parking area. Note that the start of the trail has been rerouted from that shown on the 1964 Snowdon Peak map and now heads around the west side of the lake before going uphill from the southwest corner of the lake. An information kiosk and sign-in point are located approximately 100 yards up this trail. The trail can be snow covered and tricky to follow, into June. After 0.7 mile, leave the Crater Lake Trail at a point where the trail swings to the southwest. Head southeast across an open meadow. Leave the meadow at mile 1.1, crossing a minor tree-covered ridge and entering a second clearing at mile 1.3. Continue southeast across the clearing with a clear view of your destination, and follow a drainage until you are able to gain a knoll at 12,090 feet, almost directly below the couloir. This may be a good place to stash snowshoes and don crampons.

THE CLIMB: Cross to the start of the couloir and head up the deeply inset snow slopes. The couloir averages around 40 degrees with a steeper section, at about two-thirds height, approaching 55 degrees. The left-hand wall offers placements for rock protection, although the amazingly compact quartzite may be more suitable for knife-blade pitons than anything else.

The walls of the couloir shield the snow from early-morning sun, but by 10 a.m. (depending on the season), the right-hand wall will be in the sun and the shedding will begin. Therefore, it is important to be alert for rockfall. Expect spontaneous rockfall from the left side, too. At the steeper section, a rock band that is covered early in the season will require some easy mixed moves later. The exit will also melt out later in the season, requiring more of the same. The summit is a short scramble from where you reach the exposed ridge; traverse below the summit to the southeast ridge.

DESCENT: If conditions allow, you may want to rappel and down climb the route. Otherwise, the easiest descent is along the northeast ridge to the top of a low-angled gully at 12,570 feet.

This traverse of the ridge may be the crux of the climb, depending on conditions. A series of ledges on the east side of the ridge just below the ridge top, and sometimes marked with cairns, lead the way down. If the route is dry, the difficulty should not exceed Class 3; however, in normal spring conditions, expect to make slow progress along the ridge to an obvious saddle at the top of the descent gully. Head down this gully, which averages around 30 degrees, back to your snowshoes, then retrace your steps to the parking area.

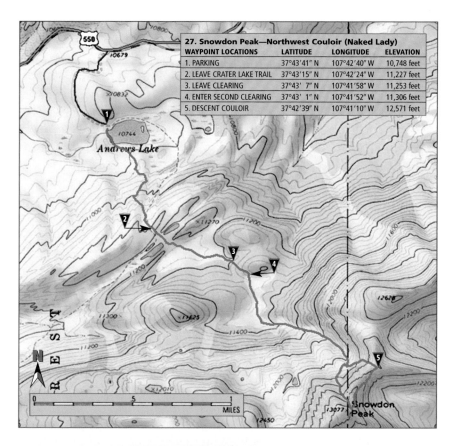

27. Snowdon Peak—Northwest Couloir (Naked Lady)			
WAYPOINT LOCATIONS	LATITUDE	LONGITUDE	ELEVATION
1. PARKING	37°43'41" N	107°42'40" W	10,748 feet
2. LEAVE CRATER LAKE TRAIL	37°43'15" N	107°42'24" W	11,227 feet
3. LEAVE CLEARING	37°43' 7" N	107°41'58" W	11,253 feet
4. ENTER SECOND CLEARING	37°43' 1" N	107°41'52" W	11,306 feet
5. DESCENT COULOIR	37°42'39" N	107°41'10" W	12,571 feet

Carefully descending the exposed ledges on Snowdon's northeast ridge.

PHOTO BY DAVE COOPER

Sunrise on a little-known gem. The north couloir on Quandary Peak sees little traffic, but provides a good moderate outing.

COLORADO SNOW CLIMBS

28. Quandary Peak— North Face Couloirs

ELEVATION GAIN	3,480 feet
ROUND-TRIP DISTANCE	7.3 miles
STARTING ELEVATION	10,920 feet
HIGHEST ELEVATION	14,265 feet
BEST MONTHS TO CLIMB	Late May through mid June
DIFFICULTY	Moderate to steep snow
GEAR	Crampons, ice ax, snowshoes, and helmet; if you decide to play around on one of the steeper exit lines, you may want to bring along a second ice tool
MAP	Breckenridge 7.5 minute

GETTING THERE: From Colorado 9, 2.4 miles north of Hoosier Pass, turn west onto Blue Lakes Road. After 0.1 mile, turn right (northeast) and follow this road for 2.1 miles to the McCullough Gulch Trailhead. In early season, this road is probably snow covered and not drivable. On May 21, 2007, it was possible to drive a little way past the summer trailhead.

COMMENT: As the season progresses and the Cristo Couloir on the south face of Quandary starts to melt out, think about venturing onto the north side of the mountain. Located immediately west of the north ridge is a moderate couloir that offers almost 2,000 vertical feet of snow. This couloir is less serious than some of the more deeply inset gullies to the east of the north ridge and provides a fun climb directly to the summit of Quandary. In late May, the cornices will probably be gone, while by mid June the upper and lower sections start to melt out. Therefore, this climb has a narrow window. Grab it while you can.

APPROACH: From the McCullough Gulch Trailhead, follow the road as it turns left immediately past the gate closure and heads uphill. When you are 0.4 mile beyond the gate, you'll pass some mine buildings on your left. The signs here leave you in no doubt that you should stay away from the buildings. Shortly after passing the buildings, the trail becomes more difficult to follow, but it generally stays in the trees on the north side of the drainage and continues to head west. A trail switchbacks up the steep, rocky area directly below the unnamed lake at 11,919 feet. It is necessary to bypass this area to the north, using a small gully. Exit to the left as soon as possible,

Looking down on the unnamed lake at 11,919 feet—the starting point for this route.

PHOTO BY DAVE COOPER

and head up gentle slopes to the lake. You are now directly below Quandary's north ridge. The couloir is immediately to the right (west) of the ridge. Find a way to cross the creek to the south side of the lake, and head up to the start of the couloir.

THE CLIMB: The couloir averages 35 degrees and has a remarkably consistent angle. It steepens at the first constriction before returning to a gentler grade. Because the couloir has several twists and turns, it isn't possible to see all the way to the top once you're on the climb. Therefore, don't be surprised when it appears to keep going forever. As you approach the exit, the couloir widens and provides options for a gentler escape to the left or a steeper finish straight or to the right (up to 50 degrees). You choose. Once you are out of the couloir proper, scramble up on a mixture of talus and snow to the summit.

DESCENT: Follow the east ridge down, staying on the ridge crest to treeline. (The summer trail isn't a good option in winter or spring, because it is routed through and under cornices that form regularly.) With snow on the ridge, the summer trail is hard to find below treeline, so some route finding below treeline will be necessary unless there is already a track.

28. Quandary Peak—North Face Couloirs			
WAYPOINT LOCATIONS	LATITUDE	LONGITUDE	ELEVATION
1. QUANDARY SUMMER TRAILHEAD	39°23' 8" N	106°3'42" W	10,907 feet
2. ROAD JUNCTION	39°23'55" N	106°4'10" W	11,050 feet
3. MCCULLOUGH GULCH TRAILHEAD	39°24' 4" N	106°4'45" W	11,101 feet
4. MINE	39°24' 8" N	106°4'58" W	11,306 feet

The rugged north face of Sundance Mountain hides an unknown bounty. With a short approach and multiple lines to climb, this is sure to become popular. PHOTO BY DAVE COOPER

29. Sundance Mountain— North Face Couloir

ELEVATION GAIN	300 feet on the approach and 700 feet of snow climbing
ROUND-TRIP DISTANCE	1.3 miles
STARTING ELEVATION	12,120 feet
HIGHEST ELEVATION	12,400 feet
BEST MONTHS TO CLIMB	June into July
DIFFICULTY	Moderate to steep snow, depending on the line climbed
MAP	Trail Ridge 7.5 minute

GETTING THERE: From Estes Park, follow signs to Rocky Mountain National Park and then to Trail Ridge Road. Take Trail Ridge Road to a small parking area on the south side of the road, 5.0 miles east of the visitor center at Fall River Pass and 1.4 miles west of the well-marked Forest Canyon Overlook. The parking area is due west of the summit of Sundance Mountain.

COMMENT: How many tourists have driven past Sundance Mountain while taking in the sights of Trail Ridge Road, never dreaming that the mountain had a rugged side? I might have included myself in this group if it hadn't been for friends (Dan Bereck and Gerry and Jennifer Roach) who climbed the peak during the winter of 2006–2007 and took photos of some great-looking snowfields cascading off of the north side.

Perhaps a little lazier than that august group, I waited until Trail Ridge Road had opened for the season (usually just before Memorial Day) before taking their advice and checking out the climbing. And what a delightful place it is. While it is one continuous snowfield in the winter, in spring and summer it takes on more character, with several interesting lines appearing.

Choose anything from wide open, moderate slopes to an intriguing narrow gully with a steep exit by a cornice.

This is the perfect place for practicing your snow-climbing skills and for teaching. With 600 to 700 feet of snow climbing at angles averaging 45 degrees, but offering short sections of 50-degree and steeper climbing, you'll want to take a couple of laps on different lines.

APPROACH: I love this approach. From the car, walk 0.5 mile up the gentle, snow-covered (early-season) slopes of Sundance Mountain, aiming for a saddle slightly left (west) of the summit. You are now at the top of the climb!

Climbing the deeply inset snow gully to climber's left of the main couloir.

From here, you can decide how to proceed. Either downclimb the gentlest line, or head for moderate slopes half a mile east of the summit and descend.

THE CLIMB: Choose a line—either the broad, central snowfield or perhaps a nice narrow gully 250 yards to the east. Better yet, climb both (after checking out the cornice at the head of the narrow gully).

DESCENT: From the top of the snowfield, head back to your car.

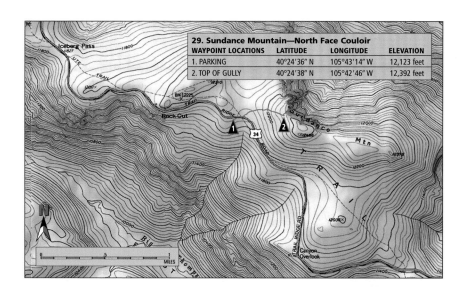

29. Sundance Mountain—North Face Couloir			
WAYPOINT LOCATIONS	LATITUDE	LONGITUDE	ELEVATION
1. PARKING	40°24′36″ N	105°43′14″ W	12,123 feet
2. TOP OF GULLY	40°24′38″ N	105°42′46″ W	12,392 feet

Winter conditions on Sundance's north face.   PHOTO BY DAN BERECK

The setting moon over the Flying Dutchman. One of several stellar climbs starting above Chasm Lake, this one lasts longer into the summer season than its neighbors.

30. Longs Peak Area— The Flying Dutchman Couloir

TOTAL ELEVATION	4,200 feet
ROUND-TRIP DISTANCE	9.7 miles
STARTING ELEVATION	9,450 feet
HIGHEST ELEVATION	13,455 feet
BEST MONTHS TO CLIMB	Late May into July
DIFFICULTY	Steep snow with a short 25- to 30-foot section of WI2-3; if the ice is not fully formed, then this section would offer easy mixed climbing (M2-3)
GEAR	Crampons, two ice tools, and helmet; most climbers will protect at least the crux ice/mixed section, so a rope, a small alpine rack, plus 2 short ice screws would be a good idea
MAP	Longs Peak 7.5 minute

GETTING THERE: Drive north from Lyons on Colorado 7 from its junction with Colorado 36 for 25.1 miles, or go south on Colorado 7 for 9.2 miles from its intersection with Colorado 36 in Estes Park. Turn west at the sign for Longs Peak Area, and drive 1.1 miles to park at the Longs Peak Ranger Station. Rocky Mountain National Park fees are not collectted at this location.

COMMENT: This excellent climb combines mainly snow with a short (25- to 30-foot) section of easy ice or mixed climbing. The views of the Diamond from high up on this climb are outstanding, as are the views of the Loft. The climb is located above the southwest corner of Chasm Lake and is immediately left of Lambs Slide. Because of its sheltered location, the snow can remain into the summer months.

APPROACH: From the parking area at the ranger station, follow the Longs Peak Trail to Chasm Lake for 4.2 miles (staying left at the Granite Pass turnoff on the Mills Moraine), until the trail peters out in a meadow by the ranger hut. As always, proceed carefully across the snowfield above Peacock Pool. Especially in the morning, the slopes can be icy. From the ranger hut, scramble west up to Chasm Lake. If the lake is well frozen, walk straight across the ice or skirt the left edge of the lake. If this isn't possible, then scramble around the right side of the lake and cut back over to the lake's southwest corner.

Thirty feet of ice climbing spices up this route.   PHOTO BY DAVE COOPER

THE CLIMB: From the lake, start up the obvious gully on moderate snow slopes. The climb averages 38 degrees as it gains 1,300 feet of elevation, but it reaches 60 degrees in the crux section. Watch for rockfall. We saw a little when we climbed the route on June 8, 2007.

Straightforward snow climbing takes you to the crux, where the gully narrows at the rock step. If this section is coated with a good layer of ice, it can be a straightforward climb, protectable with short ice screws. Often, though, the ice is either not continuous or is not well bonded to the rock, so a little mixed climbing might be necessary.

Above the crux section, continue to climb snow up to the junction with Lambs Slide. Take a break and look to your right for great views of the east face of Longs.

Continue up on easier terrain, and angle left to exit the gully above the Loft. You will have more good views over to Meeker and the Flying Buttress from here.

DESCENT: The best descent is to head right over to the Loft and find the ramp that bypasses the rock/ice step at the top of the Loft. The ramp is located on the south side of the Loft, and the climbers' trail to the top of the ramp is marked with cairns. Carefully downclimb the ramp back into the Loft, where the slope is now moderate. Either glissade or down climb the snowfield and head back to the ranger hut. Then retrace your steps along the trail back to the Mills Moraine, then down the Longs Peak Trail to the parking area.

One thing to watch for is ice falling off of the rock slabs on Mount Lady Washington as you cross the snowfield above Peacock Pool.

Above the ice/mixed section. Chasm Lake can be seen below.   PHOTO BY DAVE COOPER

SEE MAP PAGE 139

Superstar presents a stunning appearance when seen from the shoulder of James Peak on the approach. Note the sizeable cornice that we were able to avoid by climbing mixed ground just left of the main gully. PHOTO BY DAVE COOPER

31. James Peak—
Northeast Face Couloirs
(Featuring Shooting Star and Superstar)

ELEVATION GAIN	3,250 feet
ROUND-TRIP DISTANCE	7.5 miles
STARTING ELEVATION	10,400 feet
HIGHEST ELEVATION	13,294 feet
BEST MONTHS TO CLIMB	June through July
DIFFICULTY	Very steep snow with a mixed finish or rock finishes in the 5.4 to 5.7 range to avoid the cornice
GEAR	Crampons, two ice tools, and helmet; the exit from this climb is technical, so a rope and a small alpine rack will be necessary
MAP	Empire 7.5 minute

GETTING THERE: Take the Fall River Road exit (exit 238) from Interstate 70, approximately 1.2 miles west of Idaho Springs. Drive generally northwest on Fall River Road for 9.1 miles to a small parking area on your left, just past the signed start to the St. Mary's Glacier Trail. The large parking area immediately before the trailhead is no longer available for public parking. Also, if you park along the road, you are likely to be ticketed.

COMMENT: Standing in the basin below the rugged northeast face of James Peak as the sun rises is one of the quintessential alpine experiences in Colorado. Several snow lines exist on this face, but two of them stand out. Shooting Star takes a steep and very direct line to the summit, while to the right, Superstar aims for a point high on the north ridge.

There is usually only a small cornice on the northern edge of the Shooting Star exit, while the cornice above Superstar is large and threatening. Make sure to climb Superstar on a day when the cornice is unlikely to fall off. Getting caught below it would definitely ruin your day.

As on any couloir climb, take a few minutes as you gear up to observe the face for rockfall. Shooting Star seems to be more prone to this than Superstar, so it is especially important to be efficient in moving up the climb.

Bypassing the cornice on mixed terrain immediately left of the main gully, starting on a left-trending loose rock ramp before heading up to a weakness in the cornice.

PHOTO BY MEREDITH LAZAROFF

APPROACH: There are several ways to approach the east face of James Peak, and none are trivial. I've found the most reliable to be from St. Mary's Glacier. If snow conditions are good, it is possible to traverse directly into the basin at the base of the climbs, avoiding the loss of elevation entailed by the alternate route. Once the snow has melted off the slopes, this traverse becomes quite ugly, being on loose talus. Under these conditions, it is better to bite the bullet and descend using the climbers' trail also described here.

From the parking area, walk back 200 yards down the road to the start of the old jeep road signed to St. Mary's Glacier. The trail heads up the jeep road, taking the left fork (uphill) after 200 yards, and again taking the left fork in a further 150 yards. Continue on the trail to St. Mary's Lake, a total of 0.6 mile from the car.

The glacier starts at the far end of the lake. Head for the right side of the glacier and walk northwest up the gentle slopes of the glacier until you top out on the broad expanse of the flats in front of James Peak.

From the upper reaches of the glacier, you will have your first view of James Peak. Depending on the snow cover, you may find a trail, periodically marked by giant cairns, leading across the flats toward James Peak. Aim for the broad east shoulder of James Peak.

If you look closely at the rugged face on the peak's right side, you can see the top of Superstar, guarded at the very top by the impressive cornice.

For the direct traverse to the base of the climbs, head up to a point on the east ridge of James Peak at about 12,300 feet. If the traverse is covered with firm snow, this is a nice way to go. A third of a mile of traversing brings you to a shoulder overlooking the basin at the base of the climbs. Down-climb off of this shoulder and head for the flat area that makes a good spot to gear up.

If the traverse described above doesn't look inviting, a climbers' trail can be used to drop down to James Peak Lake. This trail starts at a small rock rib on the north side of the broad east shoulder of James Peak at an elevation of 12,000 feet. Lose elevation quickly on this loose trail, contour to the left edge of the lake, and continue until it is possible to climb west on snow slopes leading to the basin below the climbs.

THE CLIMB: Both climbs described here have a common start, so head up to the base of the Y at about 12,700 feet, where the climbs split.

To climb Shooting Star, take the left branch. The route climbs steeply on snow for 600 feet at an average angle of 47 degrees, with sections that are somewhat steeper. A bergschrund near the start of the climb can become increasingly difficult to negotiate as the snow melts out.

A rock bench on the left about halfway up can provide a place for you to catch your breath. From here, climb up the steepening snow to the spectacular exit, where you emerge onto the flats only a few feet away from the summit.

High on Shooting Star. PHOTO BY KEVIN CRAIG

Approaching the east face of James Peak. Shooting Star is the left branch of the obvious Y, while Superstar heads right.   PHOTO BY KEVIN CRAIG

For Superstar, take the obvious right-leaning branch from the Y. Climb up steepening snow for 300 feet to a point about 20 feet below the cornice. We found better rock anchors on the right side of the gully. A bergschrund perhaps 50 feet below the cornice can require care to cross. The angle in the couloir averages 53 degrees, with the upper part approaching 60 degrees. Friends report exits on the rock rib to the right of the gully in the 5.7 range, plus easier but still technical lines further right. Use the right-angling snow bench below the rib to gain these.

We found a very aesthetic mixed line to the left of the snow that offered a more direct exit, but before taking this line, carefully examine the state of the cornice, which should be essentially melted out above this left side.

From the belay 20 feet below the cornice, move to the left side of the snow and climb a left-angling rock ramp with some loose rock for 20 feet to a rib. Climb the rib on moderate, mixed terrain that doesn't offer much protection, due to the fractured nature of the rock. When we climbed this route on June 13, 2007, fresh snow on the ledges contributed to the difficulty of finding gear placements.

When you reach the cornice remnant, look for a break that allows you to exit onto the flats. Find one or more large rocks to sling for an anchor. Continue up the gentle north ridge to the summit.

DESCENT: From the summit, follow the trail on the east slopes back down the gentle ridge, and head back to St. Mary's Glacier. Make sure to choose the correct drainage to descend. The rocky point just above the glacier makes a good reference point toward which to head.

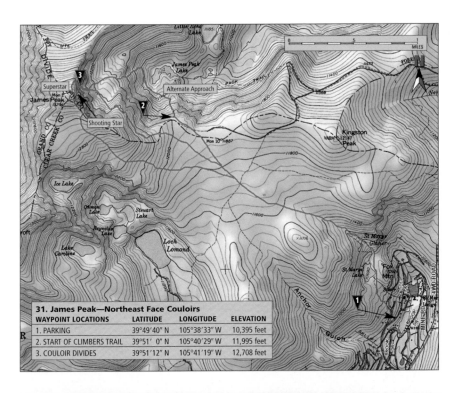

31. James Peak—Northeast Face Couloirs			
WAYPOINT LOCATIONS	LATITUDE	LONGITUDE	ELEVATION
1. PARKING	39°49'40" N	105°38'33" W	10,395 feet
2. START OF CLIMBERS TRAIL	39°51' 0" N	105°40'29" W	11,995 feet
3. COULOIR DIVIDES	39°51'12" N	105°41'19" W	12,708 feet

Starting up Shooting Star.

The dominant couloir on the north face of North Twilight Peak. The left branch offers a moderate climb, while the direct finish provides more of a challenge. PHOTO BY DAVE COOPER

32. North Twilight Peak— North Face Couloirs

ELEVATION GAIN	3,240 feet
ROUND-TRIP DISTANCE	13.6 miles
STARTING ELEVATION	10,172 feet
HIGHEST ELEVATION	13,397 feet
BEST MONTHS TO CLIMB	June into July; late May can provide good conditions but the approach can be difficult
DIFFICULTY	Moderate or steep snow, depending on the line chosen
GEAR	Crampons, ice ax and a second tool (or 2 tools), snowshoes (in early season), and helmet; a rope and small rock rack might be useful, depending on the line chosen, conditions, and comfort level
MAP	Snowdon Peak 7.5 minute

GETTING THERE: From Silverton, take U.S. 550 south for 6.4 miles to the summit of Molas Pass. Continue south for a further 0.9 mile to the Andrews Lake road. Turn left and follow the paved road for 0.7 mile to a parking area at Andrews Lake.

COMMENT: The north face of North Twilight Mountain is a mountaineer's dream in spring and early summer. Arrayed across the face are any number of enticing snow lines, from broad, moderate couloirs that call out to be skied to steep lines no more than three feet wide containing a mixture of snow and ice. Combine this with a climb of the Naked Lady couloir on Snowdon for a great road trip.

On the Crater Lake approach, you will have good views of the face, dominated by the main couloir that cuts right to left across the face to exit just left of the summit. This moderate couloir is a favorite among skiers and also makes a good climb. A direct line that diverges to the right of the main couloir is perhaps the best climb on the face. This line also bifurcates, offering several options depending on snow and cornice conditions. The latter lines reach the summit ridge just right of the summit. One of these is the route I will describe here.

One bonus of climbing North Twilight Peak is the unequalled views of the Needles and Grenadiers, seen across the intervening void of the Animas River canyon.

Due to the length of the approach, and especially in May (even on the

Approaching North Twilight. The narrow finger of snow referred to in the text can be seen at the far left end of the ridge. PHOTO BY DAVE COOPER

Memorial Day weekend) with snow on the trail, you might consider a camp near Crater Lake. There are few places more scenic, and the difficulty of finding and staying on the trail when it is snow covered can add significantly to the time required for this approach.

APPROACH: From the trailhead by Andrews Lake, follow the trail for 5.1 miles as it winds its way to Crater Lake, with a few ups and downs along the way. Note that the trail begins on the west side of Andrews lake, not on the east side, as shown on topographic maps.

From Crater Lake, head west to the base of the broad couloir below the summit. Be careful not to head up one of the other routes unless that is your plan.

THE CLIMB: The climb starts above the moraine on moderate terrain. Depending on the exit you choose, the route climbs around 1,300 feet at an average angle of 35 degrees. If you take the direct line over the cornice remnant, expect to find snow to 50 degrees. To do this finish, stay right at the first split and head directly up to the cornice (which you should have inspected before committing). Another split a little before the exit cornice offers lines to the left. If you choose the major left-hand variation that exits to the left of the summit, expect to find snow to 40 degrees.

With so many other good-looking lines on the face, you may want to explore some. One that is particularly nice is at the far east end of the face. From below, look for an obvious X where two snow lines cross. The line that starts on the right and crosses to the left is especially tempting. Narrowing to 3 feet in width in its upper third and with a mixture of snow and ice (the conditions I found on June 19, 2007), the upper section is quite sustained with an angle of 45 degrees or more.

DESCENT: Either descend the broad couloir that exits just east of the summit or head down the normal route, along the east ridge to the northeast shoulder. For the latter, follow the climbers' trail along or slightly to the south of the ridge, crossing some Class 3 terrain. Immediately after the northeast shoulder joins the east ridge, take the first grassy gully down, paralleling the shoulder. The trail is marked with cairns. Descend back to Crater Lake and head down the trail.

Exploring the narrow finger of snow and ice that provides an interesting alternative route.

PHOTO BY DAN STRIGHT

Moderate and fun climbing up the main section of the north couloir leads to a steeper finish.

PHOTO BY DAVE COOPER

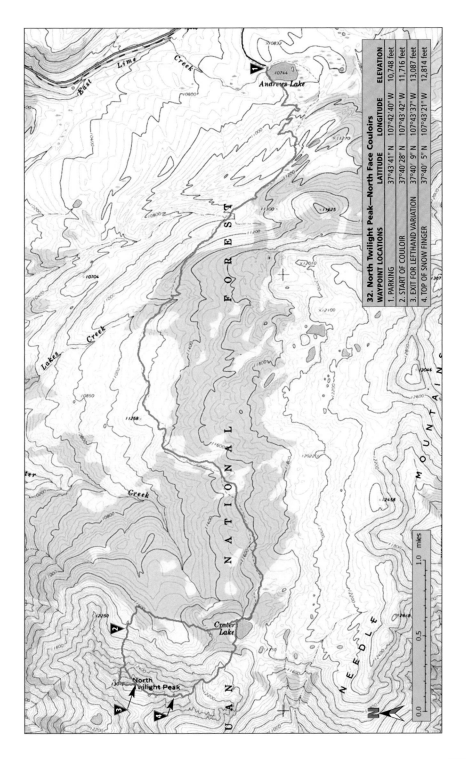

32. North Twilight Peak—North Face Couloirs

WAYPOINT LOCATIONS	LATITUDE	LONGITUDE	ELEVATION
1. PARKING	37°43'41" N	107°42'40" W	10,748 feet
2. START OF COULOIR	37°40'28" N	107°43'42" W	11,716 feet
3. EXIT FOR LEFTHAND VARIATION	37°40' 9" N	107°43'37" W	13,087 feet
4. TOP OF SNOW FINGER	37°40' 5" N	107°43'21" W	12,814 feet

Potosi Peak seen from Teakettle. The stunning snow line in the photo is the north couloir, which climbs from the Weehawken drainage to a saddle just below the summit.

COLORADO SNOW CLIMBS

33. Potosi Peak—North Couloir

ELEVATION GAIN	3,200 feet if descending the standard route; 3,600 feet if descending by reversing the ascent route
ROUND-TRIP DISTANCE	3.7 miles if descending the standard route; 3.6 miles if reversing the ascent route
STARTING ELEVATION	11,350 feet
HIGHEST ELEVATION	13,786 feet
BEST MONTHS TO CLIMB	June through mid July
DIFFICULTY	Steep snow
GEAR	Crampons, ice ax and a second tool, and helmet
MAPS	Ironton 7.5 minute Telluride 7.5 minute

GETTING THERE: From the town of Ouray, head south on U.S. 550 for 0.3 mile from the south end of Main Street, and turn right onto the Camp Bird Mine road. Cross the upper bridge over the Box Canyon at 0.4 mile, and continue on the dirt road up Canyon Creek to a junction at 4.9 miles (9,620 feet). Take the right fork, and head up Sneffels Creek to a parking area after 8.3 miles, at 11,350 feet. Note that the road becomes progressively rougher as you proceed, and to drive to the parking area mentioned definitely requires a four-wheel-drive vehicle. There is a composting outhouse at the parking area.

COMMENT: For 10 years, Gary Neben had the cover from an old *Trail and Timberline* magazine pinned to his wall. The photo on the cover featured a stunning snow couloir on the north side of Potosi, seen from Teakettle. I had first noticed this same snow couloir while on Teakettle Mountain back in 1996 and, like Gary, made a mental note to check it out at some future date.

It wasn't until Memorial Day 2006 that I planned a trip to the San Juans that would include a reconnaissance of the climb, but a near epic day prior to the planned climb caused our enthusiasm to wane temporarily. Thus, it wasn't until 2007 that we finally were able to get on the climb. A new photo taken by Charlie Winger spurred both Gary and me into action, so along with Kevin Craig, we planned our trip.

With no available information on the route, choosing an approach was non-trivial, but after closely examining the map, it became obvious that the only reasonable way to approach the climb was to descend into the Weehawken drainage from the saddle between Potosi and Teakettle's

The view from the saddle, with Teakettle in the background. From here it's a short snow climb to the summit.

PHOTO BY DAVE COOPER

subpeak, known as "Coffeepot." This would allow us to descend via the "normal" route on Potosi and return to our starting point in a one-day trip.

It turns out that, with snow, the couloir is superb and may well be the best route of any up Potosi and probably the most efficient descent line, too, avoiding the tedious traverse around the summit block on the descent.

Be aware that, especially when it is snow-covered, the "normal" route optionally used for the descent can be challenging to follow. This is one case in which it is advantageous to have climbed up the route before attempting to descend it.

APPROACH: A cliff band and evil willows make it inadvisable to head straight up from the parking area. The best line that we have found is to walk back down the road for 50 yards until a steep, grassy ramp can be accessed. This left-trending ramp will bypass the cliffs and put you in position to climb up the shallow basin south of Teakettle, staying on the grass and scree-covered rib on the right side of the basin.

Where the grade eases at around 12,000 feet, start to make an ascending traverse right into a second shallow basin below the "Coffeepot." Ascend this basin (better when snow-covered) to 13,200 feet, where a flat area below the summit towers leads to the right. Contour across the base of these towers to the "Coffeepot"–Potosi saddle.

A variation of this route that friends found is to start the traverse to the saddle a couple of hundred feet lower on obvious grassy slopes, avoiding any elevation loss along the way.

Descend from the saddle (13,000 feet) on snow into the Weehawken drainage, down to the 12,600-foot level, crossing immediately below a rock buttress on the right (west) side of the main couloir.

THE CLIMB: Start up the couloir, which averages a little more than 40 degrees for almost a thousand feet. We found it necessary to stay to the left side of the couloir to avoid numerous small rocks falling from the right-hand face, which receives early-morning sun. Also, the snow to the left will tend to be firmer, since it is shaded.

The climbing is always moderate, with only short sections higher up reaching 45 to 50 degrees. The top of the couloir is reached quite abruptly, at a small col that offers access to the summit slopes on the east face of the peak. These broad slopes, snow-covered in June, provide a fitting finish to the climb, which ends on a surprisingly large, flat summit.

DESCENT: Return down the east slopes to the col and decide on your descent route. Either reverse the route down the couloir, or use the standard ascent

Nearing the top.

PHOTO BY DAVE COOPER

route. For the latter, continue down the east slopes for perhaps 100 feet. Look for a cairn leading to the right around the east ridge as you descend.

It may be possible to follow more cairns on the descending traverse of the southeast face. Look for a gully at the 13,480-foot level that allows descent to a broad bench below. If you miss the gully, you will end up above a 50-foot vertical drop and will need to backtrack perhaps 100 feet.

Contour southwest at the 13,400-foot level and round the south ridge, then cross the southwest face, staying high to avoid cutting through the middle of the snow slope. When possible, a little way before reaching Potosi's northwest ridge, start a descending traverse back to the Potosi–"Coffeepot" saddle. Note that, without snow on the route, a slightly easier traversing route may be found.

Several options to descend from the saddle exist, most of them quite ugly. Complex cliff bands guard the direct line from the saddle down to the parking area, and while it is possible to navigate through these cliff bands, the potential for getting cliffed-out is significant. Friends report some epic descents of this face.

A safer line is to retrace your steps over to the shallow couloir on the south face of Teakettle and down.

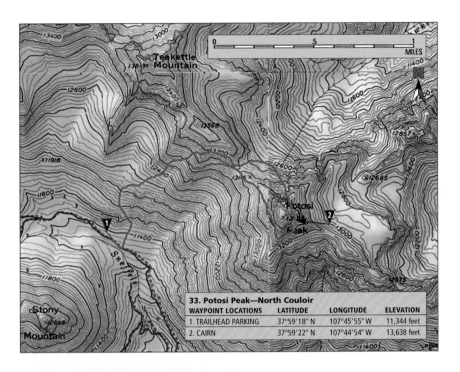

33. Potosi Peak—North Couloir

WAYPOINT LOCATIONS	LATITUDE	LONGITUDE	ELEVATION
1. TRAILHEAD PARKING	37°59′18″ N	107°45′55″ W	11,344 feet
2. CAIRN	37°59′22″ N	107°44′54″ W	13,638 feet

Starting up the couloir, head towards the left wall to minimize rockfall.

PHOTO BY DAVE COOPER

The Notch Couloir, high on the east face of Longs Peak, is reached by traversing in from the left side via Broadway.

34. Longs Peak—Notch Couloir

ELEVATION GAIN	5,500 feet
ROUND-TRIP DISTANCE	11.4 miles
STARTING ELEVATION	9,450 feet
HIGHEST ELEVATION	14,251 feet
BEST MONTHS TO CLIMB	June through July
DIFFICULTY	Steep snow, M3 mixed climbing
GEAR	Two tools, crampons, ropes (doubles make the rappel down the north face easier), helmet, alpine rock rack, and possibly a couple of ice screws
MAP	Longs Peak 7.5 minute

GETTING THERE: Drive north from Lyons on Colorado 7 from its junction with U.S. 36 for 25.1 miles, or go south on Colorado 7 for 9.2 miles from its intersection with U.S. 36 in Estes Park. Turn west at the sign for Longs Peak Area and drive 1.1 miles to park at the Longs Peak Ranger Station. Rocky Mountain National Park fees are not collected at this location.

COMMENT: A book of Colorado snow climbs simply must include the Notch Couloir. Not only is the climbing stellar, the aesthetics of this climb cannot be bettered.

Don't underestimate the commitment required for this climb. Any climb on the east face of Longs Peak is a serious undertaking, with a long approach, complex retreat, and legendary weather. In fact, weather is often the major factor determining success or failure.

While the Notch Couloir is climbed year-round, the best snow conditions are likely to occur after the couloir stops shedding snow in the spring, usually sometime after the end of May.

APPROACH: From the parking area at the ranger station, follow the Longs Peak Trail to Chasm Lake for 4.2 miles (staying left at the Granite Pass turnoff on the Mills Moraine), until the trail peters out in a meadow by the ranger hut. Prior to reaching the ranger hut, you will cross the snowfield above Peacock Pool. As always, proceed carefully across the snowfield, especially in the morning when the slopes can be icy. From the ranger hut, scramble west up to Chasm Lake. If the lake is well frozen, walk straight across the ice or scramble around the right side of the lake and head over to the base of Lambs Slide.

Making the exposed moves past one of the difficulties on Broadway.
PHOTO BY DAVE COOPER

THE CLIMB: Climb Lambs Slide for 700 feet. The snow averages 42 degrees and can be icy or avalanche prone. If you are concerned about conditions, it is possible to protect this section using rock pro on the right side. Of course, if avalanche conditions are suspect here, then perhaps you should think twice about climbing the Notch Couloir.

Exit to the right onto Broadway, the ramp that divides the east face in two. Depending on the amount of snow on Broadway and your tolerance for exposure, you may want to protect the traverse to the start of the Notch Couloir. There are a couple of tricky sections to navigate on this traverse. The first is a short downclimb not far from the beginning of Broadway, and the second is the narrow ledge guarded by an overhang shortly before you reach the start of the couloir. This latter obstacle is often negotiated by crawling under the overhang.

Once you are in the couloir, climb about 400 vertical feet to a constriction. Conditions will vary widely along the whole climb. We found a short rock section some distance below the constriction when climbing the route in late June, then ice in the constriction. Above the constriction, the route doglegs to the right and heads over another rock/ice section that may be the crux of the route.

Above this, the route turns to the left and heads directly for the Notch. This section can also contain ice. Rock pro works well and ice screws are often not necessary.

The Notch is a remarkable place, sitting near the top of the east face with Chasm Lake 2,200 feet below, while Keplingers Couloir drops off to the west. The views of the Palisades are also spectacular.

To continue on to the summit of Longs Peak, the easiest route is to join the Clarks Arrow/Keplingers Couloir route and scramble west, then north, to join the Homestretch on the normal route.

If the weather is threatening, it may be better to head in the other direction, toward the Loft past Clarks Arrow and back down to the trail below Chasm Lake.

A third alternative is to climb directly to the summit of Longs via the southeast ridge (reportedly between 5.0 and 5.5, depending on the route taken).

DESCENT: Descend via the Cables Route (route 8).

Belaying up to the Notch, with Chasm Lake 2,200 feet below.   PHOTO BY KEVIN CRAIG

SEE MAP PAGE 81

The remote east face of Ypsilon Mountain. Both the righthand branch of the Y-Couloir and the upper part of of the left branch can be seen in this photo.

PHOTO BY DAVE COOPER

35. Ypsilon Mountain—East Face (Featuring Y-Couloir, Left Branch)

ELEVATION GAIN	4,600 feet from Chapin Pass; 5,400 feet from the Lawn Lake Trailhead
ROUND-TRIP DISTANCE	8.6 miles from Chapin Pass; 11.6 miles from the Lawn Lake Trailhead
STARTING ELEVATION	11,000 feet at Chapin Pass; 8,550 feet at the Lawn Lake Trailhead
HIGHEST ELEVATION	13,514 feet
BEST MONTHS TO CLIMB	July
DIFFICULTY	Very steep snow, possibly some ice (AI3) and rock (5.0 or harder); this route should be attempted only by experienced climbers
GEAR	Crampons, ice ax, and a second tool in early season; later, 2 ice tools can be useful; alpine rock rack; at least a short length of rope; helmet
MAP	Trail Ridge 7.5 minute

GETTING THERE: Via Chapin Pass Trailhead: Drive to the town of Estes Park. From the major intersection of U.S. 34 and 36 in Estes Park, head west through town on U.S. 36. Turn south in 0.4 mile and continue on U.S. 36 as it turns west to Rocky Mountain National Park. At 7.3 miles (Deer Ridge Junction), take the right fork on U.S. 34 and drive to the Endovalley Road junction at mile 9.1. Turn left (west) on the road signed to Endovalley and the Fall River Road, reaching the Endovalley Picnic Area at mile 11.0. You can also use the Fall River Road Entrance to the park to get here.

The Fall River Road continues from here—a single-lane, well-graded dirt road suitable for passenger cars but not for motor homes. The road climbs steeply through many tight turns to the Chapin Pass Trailhead at mile 17.9. Park in the small area on your left. On your return, since Fall River Road is one way, continue west to the junction with Trail Ridge Road and head back to Estes Park.

From the Lawn Lake Trailhead: The directions are the same as those above, except that immediately after turning off of U.S. 34 onto Endovalley Road, look for the trailhead on your right.

COMMENT: The east face of Ypsilon Mountain in the Mummy Range offers a variety of quality mountaineering challenges. The purest snow climb is the

left branch of the Y- Couloir, with almost 2,000 feet of climbing. The right branch is also a stunning climb but usually involves significantly more technical rock climbing.

There is no easy approach to the climb, which begins above the remote Spectacle Lakes, a pristine and rarely visited spot. The standard approach is via the Lawn Lake Trail—a long, strenuous day. The distance can be shortened a little by approaching from Chapin Pass, although this also is a non-trivial route and may not save you any time due to the more complex route finding required. I will describe both approaches; you choose.

No matter which way you choose to get to the climb, you'll be rewarded with a committing climb requiring good general mountaineering skills. Be prepared for anything—snow, ice, rock—and you won't be disappointed.

On July 6, the snow had melted out at about 12,700 feet, requiring some rock climbing to surmount.

PHOTO BY DAVE COOPER

Cornices threaten this route until midsummer, not only from the top of the climb but also from snow slopes to the left. Inspect these features before you commit to the climb.

APPROACH: From the Lawn Lake Trailhead: Follow the Ypsilon Lake Trail, taking the left fork at 1.2 miles, passing Chipmunk Lake after 3.7 miles, and arriving at Ypsilon Lake after 4.0 miles. From here, the trail can be difficult to follow, especially in the dark, which might be a good reason for a high camp or bivouac to allow you to check out this section of the approach in daylight.

At Ypsilon Lake, cross to the north side of the stream draining Chiquita Lake and follow it west for 0.2 mile until you reach the stream draining the Spectacle Lakes. Scramble up the left side of this stream, eventually reaching some Class 5.0 slabs that provide access to the basin containing the Spectacle Lakes.

From Chapin Pass: From the trailhead, start hiking north for a little more than one tenth of a mile to a trail junction. Turn right (east) and follow the trail signed to the summits of Chapin, Chiquita, and Ypsilon.

Six-tenths mile from the trailhead, take the right fork at a sign indicating that the trail leads to "All summits." The sign also says that the trail is unmaintained beyond this point. In fact, the trail is in quite good shape until it becomes faint near the summit of Mount Chiquita. Even then, there are plenty of cairns to keep you on route.

The trail emerges above treeline and traverses across the face of a minor summit named Mount Chapin (12,454 feet). Continue toward the summit of Mount Chiquita (13,069 feet), or contour to the left of the summit.

The trail descends a little less than 300 feet to the saddle with Ypsilon. From the saddle, find a reasonable descent route into the basin and head for a bench just right of Donner Ridge at 11,700 feet.

The finish to the left branch. The cornice could be bypassed on its right side.

PHOTO BY GINNI GREER

Climb up Donner Ridge on ledge systems, traversing right where possible to reach the ridge at around 11,800 feet. Descend Class 4 slabs and ledge systems down to the Spectacle Lakes. This can be a tricky section, and you may decide to follow the ridge down lower to find an easier line of descent. Contour around the left side of the upper lake to the start of the route.

THE CLIMB: Climb the snow cone at the northeast end of the Spectacle Lakes. At the top of the cone, the snow narrows through a rock band. This section can be snow, ice, or a waterfall. If the latter, a shower can be avoided by using ledge systems to the left. Some easy rock climbing may be encountered to exit this narrow section.

Climb 40-degree snow up to the junction of the Y. The right branch, directly above you, has a narrow slot that sometimes contains ice but usually is just wet, and can be bypassed on the left side. Take the left fork, which usually requires you to cross runnels created by snow sloughs. These runnels can be deep enough to get lost in, so choose your crossing spot carefully.

The grade increases to 60 degrees as you climb higher, and halfway up the left branch, at 12,700 feet, you are likely to encounter a rock step that

This view across the face shows additional cornices that threaten the route from climbers left.

PHOTO BY DAVE COOPER

can either be a short 5.0 move or two or, later in the season, considerably more difficult, requiring roped climbing. It is possible to bypass this rock section by exiting the couloir 100 feet below the rock step and traversing out left toward Prancer Ridge, then traversing back in above the rock step. This bypass may also require a rope.

Continue on up steep snow to the cornice (hopefully just a remnant), which can usually be skirted on its right edge. The summit is a short distance to your right.

DESCENT: If you are returning to Chapin Pass, the descent is trivial. Just follow cairns and then the trail back to Chiquita and past Chapin, then down the excellent trail to the parking area.

If you are returning to the Lawn Lake Trailhead, the easiest way down is to drop into the drainage between Ypsilon and Chiquita, possibly on snow slopes, and head down next to Donner Ridge to rejoin the trail at 10,875 feet. Follow the trail down to Ypsilon Lake, and then do the long slog back to the car.

35. Ypsilon Mountain—East Face (Y-Couloir, Left Branch)			
WAYPOINT LOCATIONS	LATITUDE	LONGITUDE	ELEVATION
1. LAWN LAKE TRAILHEAD	40°24'26" N	105°37'34" W	8,553 feet
2. YPSILON LAKE TRAIL JUNCTION	40°25'12" N	105°38' 5" W	9,259 feet
3. LEAVE TRAIL	40°26'40" N	105°40' 7" W	10,771 feet
4. CHAPIN PASS TRAILHEAD	40°26' 5" N	105°43'49" W	11,053 feet
5. TRAIL JUNCTION	40°26'12" N	105°43'45" W	11,145 feet
6. TRAIL JUNCTION TO SUMMITS	40°26' 7" N	105°43'15" W	11,489 feet

Climber on the westernmost couloir in early season conditions. This variation has the smallest threat from cornices and makes a good choice at this time of year.

PHOTO BY DAVE COOPER

36. Flattop Mountain Couloirs— "Ptarmigan Fingers"

ELEVATION GAIN	3,000 feet
ROUND-TRIP DISTANCE	8.6 miles
STARTING ELEVATION	9,462 feet
HIGHEST ELEVATION	12,324 feet
BEST MONTHS TO CLIMB	Mid June through October, with the caveat that, after the first winter snowfall, you should avoid them until the next season
DIFFICULTY	Steep snow during the summer months, becoming technical ice routes in the autumn
GEAR	Crampons, ice ax, and a second tool; helmet and possibly rope and pickets for summer conditions; in the autumn, most parties will climb these routes as technical ice climbs, using two ice tools, a rope, and ice screws
MAP	McHenrys Peak 7.5 minute

GETTING THERE: From the major intersection of U.S. 34 and 36 in the town of Estes Park, head west through town on U.S. 36, then turn south in 0.4 mile and continue on U.S. 36 as it turns west to Rocky Mountain National Park. Turn left (south) on Bear Lake Road after 4.4 miles, and drive to its terminus at the large parking area at 14 miles. Consider using the shuttle bus rather than driving to Bear Lake. For more information, go to: *http://www.nps.gov/romo/visit/shuttle.html.*

COMMENT: Tucked into the north face of Flattop Mountain, these three couloirs experience winter later than many other climbs in the area. Often not coming into shape until mid June, they offer climbing through the summer into autumn. In fact, autumn is my favorite time of year for these routes, when the snow has changed to ice, and they become moderate technical ice climbs.

A word of caution: Many years ago, a friend and I had planned a trip to climb one of these routes on an October day. An early-season snowfall the night before the climb caused us to change our climbing plans. We were horrified the next day to hear that two other climbers had decided to do the climb anyway and had been hit by an avalanche. They did not survive. Err on the side of caution.

If you're climbing these routes in the autumn, be prepared for ice

This view, from the vicinity of Grace Falls, shows the cornices threatening the two eastern variations.   PHOTO BY DAVE COOPER

conditions. Most parties will protect the route with ice screws. On one occasion, we arrived at the base of the first couloir just as a party was leaving. Apparently one climber had fallen and sustained hand injuries.

By the way, the large snowfield at the head of the drainage is Ptarmigan Glacier. This is your way out of the drainage if none of the climbs described here look doable.

APPROACH: From the Bear Lake parking lot, take the trail signed to Odessa Lake. Stay left after 0.4 mile at the turnoff to Bierstadt Lake, then stay right after 1.0 miles, where you leave the Flattop Mountain Trail and continue toward Odessa Lake.

After 3.0 miles, leave the Odessa Lake Trail, where the trail makes a sharp turn to the right. Instead, stay straight on a minor trail that continues southwest to Lake Helene. During June, you'll be on snow for the remainder of the approach. Just continue southwest into the drainage between Notchtop and Flattop mountains and arrive at the base of the first couloir (the easternmost) after 3.8 miles.

THE CLIMB: Choose the route that is just right (perhaps we should call these the Goldilocks Couloirs). The first couloir averages 38 degrees and is the gentlest of the three. The second couloir is a little steeper and shorter and averages 45 degrees, while the third averages 47 degrees and is the shortest.

The first two couloirs are often guarded by cornices until mid June, so it is best to avoid them before that. The third tends to have no cornice and may, therefore, be the best early-season choice.

Whichever route you choose, enjoy a relatively short but fun excursion that ends when you reach the flats, almost tripping over the Flattop Mountain Trail.

DESCENT: Follow the Flattop Mountain Trail back to Bear Lake.

Good alpine ice conditions on October 18.

PHOTO BY KEVIN CRAIG

SEE MAP PAGE 231

Challenger's headwall, the remnant of the cornice, provided a wonderful, almost vertical exit we climbed the route in late season conditions. Protecting with pickets is difficult, if not impossible, at this angle.

PHOTO BY DAVE COOPER

37. Rollins Pass Area— Challenger Glacier

ELEVATION GAIN	2,600 feet
ROUND-TRIP DISTANCE	11.4 miles
STARTING ELEVATION	11,290 feet
HIGHEST ELEVATION	12,200 feet
BEST MONTHS TO CLIMB	May be climbed during July and August, but my favorite season is in the autumn, September and October
DIFFICULTY	Steep snow or alpine ice (AI3)
GEAR	Crampons, ice tools, ice screws, maybe a picket or two, rope, and helmet
MAP	East Portal 7.5 minute

GETTING THERE: Drive to the small town of Rollinsville, 4.3 miles south of Nederland on Colorado 119. Drive west on County Road 16 (a gravel road) for 7.3 miles to the intersection with County Road 117. Turn right onto County Road 117 (the Rollins Pass Road), and drive 12.7 miles on this rough road to a parking area shortly before the Needles Eye Tunnel (now closed). This is 3.0 miles beyond Yankee Doodle Lake.

COMMENT: Steeper than its neighbor to the south (Skyscraper Glacier), Challenger Glacier is another fine alpine ice climb. Deeply inset into the cleft at the head of the Jasper Creek drainage, the glacier has a more northerly aspect and is a much colder place. This causes the glacier to often provide more reliable ice in the autumn. The headwall may need to be climbed directly to exit the glacier and is sometimes quite vertical.

Note: A great linkage of both Skyscraper and Challenger glaciers can be made from a camp near Betty Lake. Climb the Skyscraper Glacier, as described in climb 38, then continue north on the Corona Trail to Devils Thumb Pass. Approach and climb Challenger Glacier as described here, then follow the descent route back to your camp at Betty Lake, also as described in climb 38.

APPROACH: From the road closure just before the Needles Eye Tunnel, take an unmaintained trail up and over the ridge, heading generally north to bypass the tunnel before contouring above the road as it turns to the west on its way to Rollins Pass. At Rollins Pass, leave the road and follow the Corona Trail northwest for 3.7 miles to Devils Thumb Pass. Drop steeply east on the

Challenger Glacier in alpine ice shape.

Devils Thumb Trail for 0.4 mile to a small, unnamed lake at 11,275 feet. Find a way to traverse southeast, then south, around a cliffy area, losing as little elevation as possible as you contour into the drainage below the glacier. Pick your way through the moraine to the base of the glacier proper. Because this glacier is more deeply inset than its southern neighbor (Skyscraper Glacier), it is not readily visible on the approach until almost at the start of the climb.

THE CLIMB: Gear up and head up the glacier. The climb is approximately 550 feet high, although as it melts out it becomes somewhat shorter. The left side will probably have the icier conditions. Starting out at a moderate angle, averaging 35 degrees, the climb steepens as you gain elevation. Although it varies from year to year, the cornice remnant is definitely the crux of this climb and can be quite technical. I have climbed it on occasion when this exit was quite vertical for 20 feet or so, although it is usually possible to bypass the steepest part. But why would you?

DESCENT: Head over to the Corona Trail and walk south back to Rollins Pass.

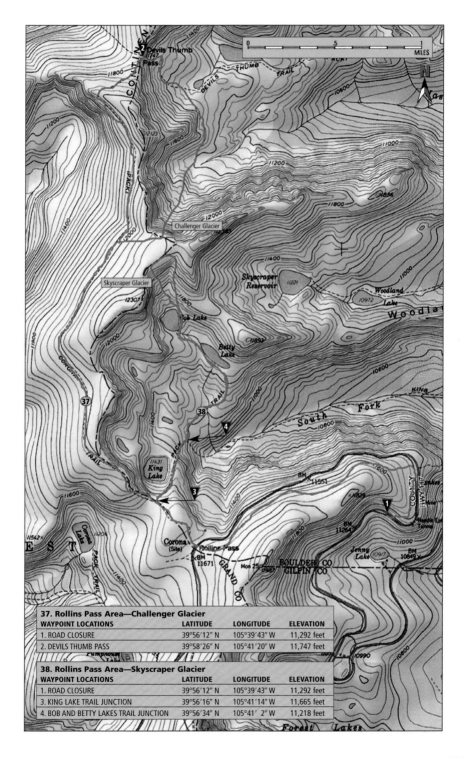

37. Rollins Pass Area—Challenger Glacier			
WAYPOINT LOCATIONS	**LATITUDE**	**LONGITUDE**	**ELEVATION**
1. ROAD CLOSURE	39°56'12" N	105°39'43" W	11,292 feet
2. DEVILS THUMB PASS	39°58'26" N	105°41'20" W	11,747 feet

38. Rollins Pass Area—Skyscraper Glacier			
WAYPOINT LOCATIONS	**LATITUDE**	**LONGITUDE**	**ELEVATION**
1. ROAD CLOSURE	39°56'12" N	105°39'43" W	11,292 feet
3. KING LAKE TRAIL JUNCTION	39°56'16" N	105°41'14" W	11,665 feet
4. BOB AND BETTY LAKES TRAIL JUNCTION	39°56'34" N	105°41' 2" W	11,218 feet

Skyscraper Glacier rises above Bob Lake, near Rollins Pass. A moderate summer snow climb, the glacier becomes technical in the autumn.   PHOTO BY DAVE COOPER

38. Rollins Pass Area— Skyscraper Glacier

ELEVATION GAIN	2,320 feet
ROUND-TRIP DISTANCE	8.2 miles
STARTING ELEVATION	11,290 feet
HIGHEST ELEVATION	12,200 feet
BEST MONTHS TO CLIMB	May be climbed during the summer months, but my favorite season is in the autumn, September and October
DIFFICULTY	Moderate snow or alpine ice (AI2)
GEAR	Crampons, ice tools, ice screws, maybe a picket or two, and helmet
MAP	East Portal 7.5 minute

GETTING THERE: Drive to the small town of Rollinsville, 4.3 miles south of Nederland on Colorado 119. Drive west on County Road 16 (a gravel road) for 7.3 miles to the intersection with County Road 117. Turn right onto County Road 117 (the Rollins Pass Road), and drive 12.7 miles on this rough road to a parking area shortly before the Needles Eye Tunnel (now closed). This is 3.0 miles beyond Yankee Doodle Lake.

COMMENT: One of the drift glaciers near Rollins Pass, Skyscraper Glacier is a long-time favorite. During the summer months, the moderate slopes make this a good spot to gain experience in general snow-climbing techniques, but for a few magical weeks in the autumn, it becomes a moderate ice climb and can be climbed with ropes, placing ice screws for protection. In a good year, the cornice can still be partially intact and offers a steeper finish if you like.

APPROACH: There are a couple of options for getting to Bob and Betty lakes. One is via the King Lake Trail, starting at the town of Hessie. The other option is to come in from the Rollins Pass Road. The latter is the one I'll describe here. From the road closure just before the Needles Eye Tunnel, take an unmaintained trail up and over the ridge, heading generally north to bypass the tunnel before contouring above the road as it turns to the west on its way to Rollins Pass. As you approach the pass, you should get a good view of the glacier. At Rollins Pass, leave the road and follow the Corona Trail northwest for just over one third of a mile to the junction with the King Lake Trail. Follow the King Lake Trail as it drops down the slope and passes King Lake on its east side. Shortly after passing the lake, you will reach

Topping out on Skyscraper. Note an alternate route in the background.   PHOTO BY DAVE COOPER

another trail junction where the trail to Bob and Betty lakes takes off to the left. Continue on, passing Betty Lake on the southwest side and then passing Bob Lake on the east side. Head up talus to the edge of the snowfield.

THE CLIMB: Choose a line that looks good on the wide expanse of snow. The glacier averages around 30 degrees but provides steeper exit options. Depending on the year, the exit on the left side of the glacier may tempt you with a cornice remnant that can provide a good, steep exit. This exit can approach the vertical for 20 feet or so. Depending on conditions, you can probably choose either a snow line or alpine ice. Wherever you top out on the glacier, you'll need to scramble up a bit of scree to reach the flats.

DESCENT: Either descend the glacier or walk northeast 0.1 mile to a grassy slope at the east margin of the glacier. From here, it is a simple walk back to the base of the glacier.

Another possibility, especially if you haven't left any gear at the base of the climb, is to head over to the Corona Trail and walk to the south directly to Rollins Pass.

Roped team travel on the glacier.

PHOTO BY DAVE COOPER

SEE MAP PAGE 211

The Fair Glacier rises to the left of Lone Eagle Peak in this photo. The approach to the glacier skirts around the base of the peak on grassy ledges.

39. Apache Peak—
Fair Glacier and
Queens Way Couloir

ELEVATION GAIN	6,000 feet
ROUND-TRIP DISTANCE	15.3 miles
STARTING ELEVATION	10,500 feet
HIGHEST ELEVATION	13,441 feet
BEST MONTHS TO CLIMB	June and July
DIFFICULTY	Moderate to steep snow
GEAR	Crampons, ice ax, and helmet
MAPS	Monarch Lake 7.5 minute
	Ward 7.5 minute

GETTING THERE: Drive 12.1 miles north of Nederland (0.4 mile north of the turnoff to Ward) on Colorado 72, and turn left (west) on the road into the Indian Peaks Wilderness. Follow the signs to the Long Lake Trailhead. The Brainard Lake area is a U.S. fee area.

COMMENT: In his guide to *Colorado's Indian Peaks Wilderness Area, Classic Hikes and Climbs*, Gerry Roach says that to do this loop, you should "get in shape, leave early." Good advice, since you'll gain and lose 6,000 feet in 15.3 miles of hiking and climbing. The reward, however, is an excellent tour of Apache Peak that takes in two snow routes in one day.

The Fair Glacier, one of the Indian Peaks' permanent snowfields, sits in a stunning setting next to Lone Eagle Peak, while the Queens Way Couloir is located on the east face of Apache Peak above Isabelle Glacier.

For a shorter day than the loop described here, Queens Way makes a good ascent route for a climb of Apache Peak.

APPROACH: From the Long Lake Trailhead, hike up the well-signed trail to Pawnee Pass at 12,541 feet, then descend the west side of the pass to its intersection with the Crater Lake Trail at 9,900 feet. Follow the Crater Lake Trail south to the lake.

THE CLIMB: Follow a deteriorating trail around the left side of Crater Lake. At the easternmost point of the lake, a steep, grassy slope heads southeast to skirt around the nose of Lone Eagle Peak. A climbers' trail (the route is also used

Approaching the toe of the glacier.

for the Class 4 ascent of Lone Eagle) hugs the base of the cliffs as it heads south to a small saddle at 11,100 feet, overlooking the glacial Triangle Lake.

Contour above Triangle Lake on talus slopes to the tongue of the glacier. The glacier averages just over 30 degrees for almost 1,400 feet, with the steepest section approaching 45 degrees above the narrowest point. By late summer, a crevasse forms across this narrow section that can be a problem to negotiate. As the season progresses, the seasonal snow melts, exposing more of the permanent ice, although as of July 22, 2007, any exposed ice was easy to avoid. Take a moment at the saddle to enjoy the views before heading up Apache. The most direct way to reach the summit follows a somewhat unpleasant, loose gully on the north side of the ridge. This gully ends on the south slopes of the peak. From here, bear to the left (northeast) up easy talus to the summit.

DESCENT: From the summit, make a descending traverse northeast down moderate talus toward the head of Queens Way Couloir, which extends from Isabelle Glacier to a small ridge that forms the northern margin of Apache's east face. The head of the couloir is at 13,000 feet, almost due east of ridge point 13,270. A faint climbers' trail extends from the summit to the top of the couloir.

Descend Queens Way Couloir for 500 feet to Isabelle Glacier. The couloir, averaging 35 degrees, holds snow or ice through the summer.

From Isabelle Glacier, continue to descend snow slopes until you can join the Isabelle Glacier Trail, which takes you down to a small, unnamed lake at 11,422 feet. The trail winds its way down the South St. Vrain Creek to Isabelle Lake, and then on past Long Lake (a very long lake on the way down) to the trailhead.

Descending Queensway. The Isabelle Glacier can be seen below.   PHOTO BY DAVE COOPER

The view down the Fair Glacier. Lone Eagle Peak looks quite small from this angle, sitting to the left of Triangle Lake.

COLORADO SNOW CLIMBS

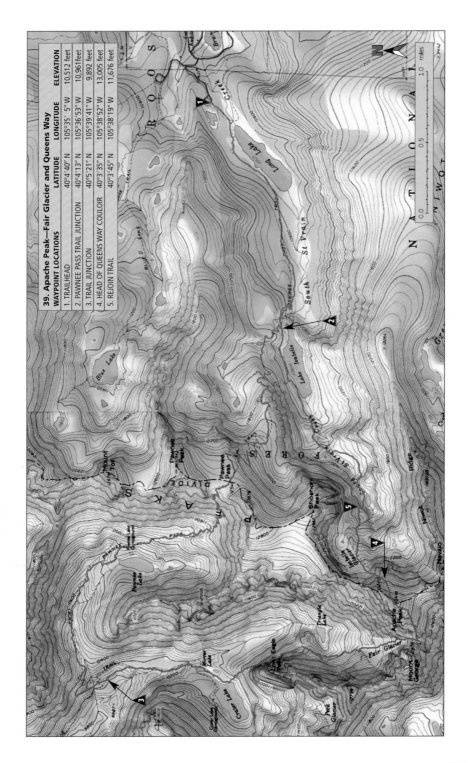

39. Apache Peak—Fair Glacier and Queens Way

WAYPOINT LOCATIONS	LATITUDE	LONGITUDE	ELEVATION
1. TRAILHEAD	40°4'40" N	105°35' 5" W	10,512 feet
2. PAWNEE PASS TRAIL JUNCTION	40°4'13" N	105°36'53" W	10,961feet
3. TRAIL JUNCTION	40°5'21" W	105°39'41" W	9,892 feet
4. HEAD OF QUEENS WAY COULOIR	40°3'35" N	105°38'52" W	13,005 feet
5. REJOIN TRAIL	40°3'45" N	105°38'19" W	11,676 feet

Taylor Glacier rises above Sky Pond at the end of Glacier Gorge. The glacier is visible during much of the approach.

40. Taylor Glacier

ELEVATION GAIN	3,960 feet
ROUND-TRIP DISTANCE	10.8 miles
STARTING ELEVATION	9,480 feet
HIGHEST ELEVATION	12,890 feet
BEST MONTHS TO CLIMB	June through October, with the best alpine ice conditions in September and October
DIFFICULTY	Very steep snow or alpine ice (AI2-3)
GEAR	In June, you may need little more than an ice ax, a few pickets, and a rope (assuming you're going to protect a part of the route); by September, it's a good idea to have two ice tools, crampons, and a few ice screws to supplement the above gear
MAP	McHenrys Peak 7.5 minute

GETTING THERE: From the major intersection of U.S. 34 and 36 in the town of Estes Park, head west through town on U.S. 36. Turn south in 0.4 mile and continue on U.S. 36 as it turns west to Rocky Mountain National Park. Turn left (south) on Bear Lake Road after 4.4 miles, and drive to the Glacier Gorge Parking Area and Trailhead, a total of 12.7 miles. Consider using the shuttle bus rather than driving to Bear Lake. For more information, go to: *http://www.nps.gov/romo/visit/shuttle.html.*

COMMENT: One of the classic alpine ice climbs in Rocky Mountain National Park, this route is always a pleasure to climb. You never know what you will find, so be prepared. On one occasion, another party was free-soloing the route ahead of us and had a rude awakening when the top of the climb turned technical and they didn't have appropriate gear. A word of caution: On one June attempt, we were chased off by a collapsing cornice when the temperature dropped suddenly. Although the climbing will generally be easier during the summer months, it certainly isn't without its hazards.

APPROACH: From the parking area, follow the signs to Loch Vale. Pass two trail junctions in the first half mile, cross a series of footbridges, and continue on to Alberta Falls. (Note that there is an unofficial climbers' trail that is regularly used as a shortcut, starting at the large split boulder by the third bridge.) Continue past the North Longs Peak trail junction, and after two miles you will reach the trail junction for Glacier Gorge. Follow the signs to Loch Vale, shortly passing another trail junction for Lake Haiyaha.

In this photo both the direct exit and the left variation (the upper of the two snow lines) are visible.

PHOTO BY DAVE COOPER

From here, the trail climbs above the drainage on its right side, reaching a series of switchbacks to avoid a cliff band. Continue on the trail up to The Loch and go around the north side. Quite a bit of trail work has recently been done in this area. The trail crosses the confluence with Andrews Creek shortly before reaching Timberline Falls. Scramble up a rock step to the right of the falls and regain the trail, which passes Glass Lake before ending at Sky Pond. Head up the moraine to the edge of the glacier, passing Sky Pond on its right-hand side.

THE CLIMB: The angle starts out moderate and steepens as you gain elevation, averaging around 36 degrees in 1,100 vertical feet. As mentioned above, the climbing is usually interesting and never predictable. A few rope lengths below the top, the climbing becomes significantly steeper, and for most people a rope becomes advisable. Depending on conditions, there are a couple of exit options. The standard exit follows the center route, which narrows down to a few feet just below the cornice guarding the exit. Some years, the cornice has to be climbed directly, sometimes on ice and sometimes on hard snow. Some years, it is possible to escape along the moat next to the cornice, as we had to do on one occasion when a wall cloud was rapidly approaching with the first winter storm of the season. Friends reported on one climb finding good water-ice conditions in the narrow exit gully below the cornice.

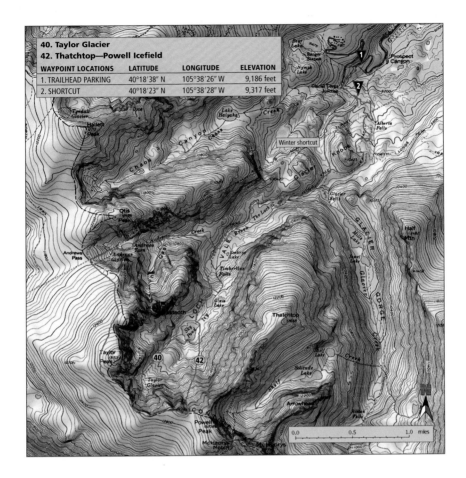

40. Taylor Glacier 42. Thatchtop—Powell Icefield			
WAYPOINT LOCATIONS	**LATITUDE**	**LONGITUDE**	**ELEVATION**
1. TRAILHEAD PARKING	40°18'38" N	105°38'26" W	9,186 feet
2. SHORTCUT	40°18'23" N	105°38'28" W	9,317 feet

Perhaps the most enjoyable climbing I've experienced was on one occasion when a friend and I found the center route to be totally melted out. A ramp to the left, a hundred feet below the top, looked interesting, so we headed that way. We found two roped pitches of technical climbing that started with thin ice over rock to a piton belay in the wall above the ramp, followed by a pitch of wonderfully steep snow (65 degrees or more) to the top. Choose one of the exits mentioned above and enjoy some fine climbing. The climb ends on the broad flats of the Continental Divide.

DESCENT: Walk north for 1.5 miles to the head of Andrews Glacier, passing Taylor Peak on the way, and descend the glacier, which is marked at its top with a sign. Once you are down the glacier, head around the south side of Andrews Tarn and continue down the trail, which is faint in places, to rejoin the Loch Vale Trail at the confluence of Icy Brook and Andrews Creek.

Nearing the top of Tyndall Glacier, on good neve. Tyndall offers excellent alpine ice in the autumn, though it can be climbed throughout the summer.   PHOTO BY CHARLIE WINGER

41. Tyndall Glacier

ELEVATION GAIN	3,000 feet
ROUND-TRIP DISTANCE	Trailhead to Tyndall Glacier, with return via the Flattop Mountain Trail, 7.4 miles
STARTING ELEVATION	9,462 feet
HIGHEST ELEVATION	12,324 feet
BEST MONTHS TO CLIMB	June through October, with the best alpine ice conditions usually found in September and October
DIFFICULTY	Steep snow or alpine ice (AI2)
GEAR	A rope, crampons and ice tools, helmet, plus a few ice screws and snow pickets should suffice
MAP	McHenrys Peak 7.5 minute

GETTING THERE: From the major intersection of U.S. 34 and 36 in the town of Estes Park, head west through town on U.S. 36. Turn south in 0.4 mile and continue on U.S. 36 as it turns west to Rocky Mountain National Park. Turn left (south) on Bear Lake Road after 4.4 miles, and drive to its terminus at the large parking area, a total of 14 miles. Consider using the shuttle bus rather than driving to Bear Lake. For more information, go to: *http://www.nps.gov/romo/visit/shuttle.html.*

COMMENT: Scattered along the east side of the Continental Divide, generally north of Interstate 70 and concentrated in the area from Rollins Pass to Rocky Mountain National Park, are a series of permanent snowfields known as drift glaciers. Formed principally by wind deposition of snow during the winter, these snowfields survive summer melting due to their protected locations. A characteristic shared by most of these drift glaciers is that, during a brief period in late summer and early autumn, before new snow falls, the surface metamorphoses into alpine ice. This has long been my favorite time of year to venture onto these glaciers, which typically offer several hundred feet of moderate ice and steep snow climbing.

A word of caution: Even a few inches of new snow on top of the alpine ice that forms in the autumn can create a significant avalanche hazard. Once it snows in the high country, it's best to leave these drift glaciers for the next year.

One fine example of a drift glacier is Tyndall Glacier in Rocky Mountain National Park. Nestled between Hallett Peak and Flattop Mountain, this glacier can be seen from many vantage points. Tyndall has some of the largest crevasses to be seen in Colorado.

Tyndall Glacier, with the vertical north face of Hallett Peak to the left.   PHOTO BY DAVE COOPER

APPROACH: From the Bear Lake Parking Area, take the left turn at the "Y" before Bear Lake, following the signs for Dream Lake and Emerald Lake. After 0.5 mile, you will reach Nymph Lake. Continue on the excellent trail as it passes Dream Lake before reaching the outlet of Emerald Lake after 1.5 miles of hiking. Once you reach Emerald Lake, there are a couple of options to reach the glacier, the goal being to bypass the cliffs directly above the lake. A reasonable route follows a climbers' trail that provides access to the north face of Hallett Peak. From the lake's eastern end, follow the rough trail as it climbs south approximately 100 vertical feet to a flatter area before turning west and contouring toward Hallett's vertical face. The trail ascends, staying close to Hallett, until it reaches the top of the cliff band at about 10,800 feet. A sizable cairn, complete with a small pole, marks this point. Head northwest toward the center of the drainage, and work your way west on rock slabs and grassy ramps—slow going all the way. Snow patches can speed progress, although in late summer most of these have melted out. Find the easiest way to surmount the moraine below the glacier.

Negotiating a crevasse, high on Tyndall.   PHOTO BY CHARLIE WINGER

THE CLIMB: Tyndall offers several pitches of good ice and snow climbing. The average steepness is around 40 degrees, depending on the line you choose. You will start out gently, with the steepest climbing just before the exit. Note the crevasses high on the face as you approach the climb, and plan a route that avoids them. The snow bridges can be quite tenuous. In general, the routes become steeper the farther left you go. Choose your route and head up.

The dark-colored part of the glacier is alpine ice and can be protected with ice screws, but it is usually helpful to have pickets along for the snow-covered sections. Expect to find water running over the surface of the ice as the day warms. Most parties will prefer the security of a rope on the steeper part of the glacier, and, with good alpine ice conditions, two ice tools and crampons are generally required.

Climbers on Tyndall. The black ice seen on the lower part of the climb was running with water on this day.   PHOTO BY CHARLIE WINGER

Topping out, in this photo from the early '90s. A photo of a good climb with good friends brings back lots of memories.

PHOTO BY CHARLIE WINGER

DESCENT: As you top out, you will be very close to the trail heading over to Flattop Mountain. Take this trail north over the broad summit, and continue down the well-marked and well-worn Flattop Mountain Trail as it heads generally east, descending back to Bear Lake. At the trail junction shortly before Bear Lake, the trail signs should keep you on track.

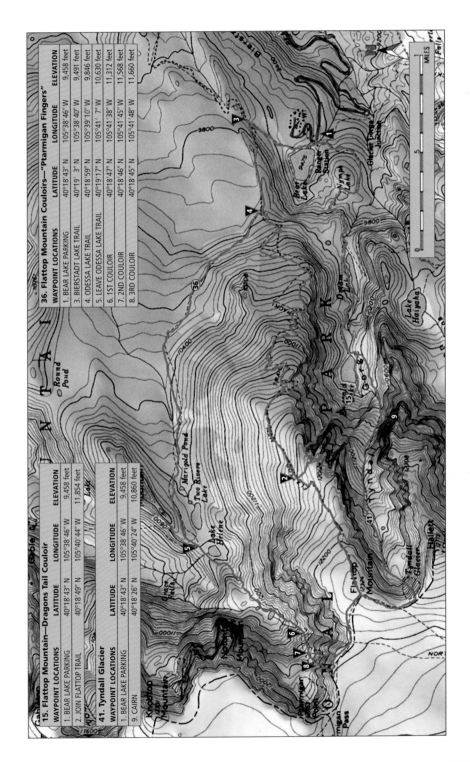

15. Flattop Mountain—Dragons Tail Couloir

WAYPOINT LOCATIONS	LATITUDE	LONGITUDE	ELEVATION
1. BEAR LAKE PARKING	40°18'43" N	105°38'46" W	9,458 feet
2. JOIN FLATTOP TRAIL	40°18'49" N	105°40'44" W	11,854 feet

41. Tyndall Glacier

WAYPOINT LOCATIONS	LATITUDE	LONGITUDE	ELEVATION
1. BEAR LAKE PARKING	40°18'43" N	105°38'46" W	9,458 feet
9. CAIRN	40°18'26" N	105°40'24" W	10,860 feet

36. Flattop Mountain Couloirs—"Ptarmigan Fingers"

WAYPOINT LOCATIONS	LATITUDE	LONGITUDE	ELEVATION
1. BEAR LAKE PARKING	40°18'43" N	105°38'46" W	9,458 feet
3. BIERSTADT LAKE TRAIL	40°19' 3" N	105°38'40" W	9,491 feet
4. ODESSA LAKE TRAIL	40°18'59" N	105°39'10" W	9,846 feet
5. LEAVE ODESSA LAKE TRAIL	40°19'17" N	105°41' 7" W	10,630 feet
6. 1ST COULOIR	40°18'47" N	105°41'38" W	11,312 feet
7. 2ND COULOIR	40°18'46" N	105°41'45" W	11,568 feet
8. 3RD COULOIR	40°18'45" N	105°41'48" W	11,660 feet

The Thatchtop-Powell Ice Field provides steep to very steep snow and alpine ice. The snow to the right of the rock rib offers the steepest exit, approaching 70 degrees.

42. Thatchtop—Powell Ice Field

ELEVATION GAIN	4,150 feet
ROUND-TRIP DISTANCE	11.2 miles
STARTING ELEVATION	9,480 feet
HIGHEST ELEVATION	12,970 feet
BEST MONTHS TO CLIMB	The best alpine ice conditions occur in September and October; earlier in the summer, the face is susceptible to avalanching; once fresh snow covers the ice in the autumn, the slope can be very unstable
DIFFICULTY	Very steep snow or alpine ice (AI3)
GEAR	Two ice tools, crampons, a rope, and a few ice screws in addition to a couple of pickets
MAP	McHenrys Peak 7.5 minute

GETTING THERE: From the major intersection of U.S. 34 and 36 in the town of Estes Park, head west through town on U.S. 36. Turn south in 0.4 mile and continue on U.S. 36 as it turns west to Rocky Mountain National Park. Turn left (south) on Bear Lake Road after 4.4 miles, and drive to the Glacier Gorge Parking Area and Trailhead, a total of 12.7 miles. Consider using the shuttle bus rather than driving to Bear Lake. For more information, go to: *http://www.nps.gov/romo/visit/shuttle.html.*

COMMENT: Located in Loch Vale, to the left of its better-known neighbor, the Taylor Glacier, the Thatchtop-Powell Ice Field is perhaps the steepest of the drift glaciers. It is often not safe to climb until late summer or early autumn, since it has the reputation for avalanching until then. In September and October, you are likely to find good ice conditions and technical climbing for which most people will want a rope. Because the ice field offers a choice of lines, you should be able to find one that meets your needs.

APPROACH: From the parking area, follow the signs to Loch Vale. Pass two trail junctions in the first half mile, cross a series of footbridges, and continue on to Alberta Falls. (Note that there is an unofficial climbers' trail that is regularly used as a shortcut, starting at the large split boulder by the third bridge.) Continue on past the North Longs Peak Trail junction, and after 2 miles you will reach the trail junction for Glacier Gorge. Follow the signs to Loch Vale, shortly passing another trail junction for Lake Haiyaha. From here, the trail climbs above the drainage on its right side, reaching a series of switchbacks to avoid a cliff band. Continue on the trail up to The

This view from Flattop Mountain provides an unusual view of the Icefield.   PHOTO BY DAVE COOPER

Loch and go around the north side. Quite a bit of trail work has recently been done in this area. The trail crosses the confluence with Andrews Creek shortly before reaching Timberline Falls. Scramble up a rock step to the right of the falls and regain the trail, which passes Glass Lake before ending at Sky Pond. From Sky Pond, head south on talus slopes, angling toward the base of the obvious snowfield. The small cliff bands below the climb are easily avoided.

THE CLIMB: This one starts out steep and gets steeper. Generally, the broad slopes to the left are less steep. A narrower finger of snow on the right margin of the snowfield just to the right of a rock rib offers the steepest climbing, with an angle exceeding 65 degrees near the top. When I first climbed this route in October 1997, I chose to belay the last couple of pitches of this right-most variation. This is definitely one of the finest alpine ice climbs in the park, providing up to 1,000 feet of great climbing.

DESCENT: Walk west and then north for 2 miles, passing Taylor Peak on the way, to the head of Andrews Glacier. Descend here. The top of the glacier is marked with a sign. Once you are down the glacier, head around the south side of Andrews Tarn and continue down the trail, which is faint in places, to rejoin the Loch Vale Trail at the confluence of Icy Brook and Andrews Creek.

Topping out on the righthand variation.   PHOTO BY DAVE COOPER

SEE MAP PAGE 225

The author enjoying perfect snow conditions.

PHOTO BY GINNI GREER

BIBLIOGRAPHY

Cox, Steven M. and Fulsaas, Kris, eds. *Mountaineering: The Freedom of the Hills.* Seattle, Washington: The Mountaineers Books, 2003, pp. 35, 550.

Fredston, Jill and Fesler, Doug. *Snow Sense—A Guide to Evaluating Snow Avalanche Hazard.* Anchorage, Alaska: Alaska Mountain Safety Center, Inc., 1994.

Houston, Mark and Cosley, Kathy. *Alpine Climbing: Techniques to Take You Higher.* Seattle, Washington: The Mountaineers Books, 2004.

LaChappelle, E. R. *The ABC of Avalanche Safety.* Seattle, Washington: The Mountaineers Books, 1985.

McClung, David and Schaerer, Peter. *The Avalanche Handbook.* Seattle, Washington: The Mountaineers Books, 2006.

Roach, Gerry. *Colorado's Fourteeners: From Hikes to Climbs.* Golden, Colorado: Fulcrum Publishing, 1996, p. xvi.

Roach, Gerry and Roach, Jennifer. *Colorado's Thirteeners, 13,800 to 13,999: From Hikes to Climbs.* Golden, Colorado: Fulcrum Publishing, 2001, pp. 20–21, 63.

Roach, Gerry. *Colorado's Indian Peaks Wilderness Area: Classic Hikes and Climbs.* Golden, Colorado: Fulcrum Publishing, 1989, p. 72.

Roach, Gerry. *Rocky Mountain National Park: Classic Hikes and Climbs.* Golden, Colorado: Fulcrum Publishing, 1988.

Rossiter, Richard. *Rock & Ice Climbing Rocky Mountain National Park: The High Peaks.* Evergreen, Colorado: Chockstone Press, Inc., 1997.

Tremper, Bruce. *Staying Alive in Avalanche Terrain.* Seattle, Washington: The Mountaineers Books, 2001.

ABOUT THE AUTHOR

Born in Yorkshire, England, DAVE COOPER holds a doctorate in Physics from the University of Durham. He has spent the last twenty-seven years exploring the Colorado mountains and has climbed extensively in many of the world's great ranges, including the Andes, Himalayas, Canadian Rockies, and the Alaska Range. Dave is the author of *Colorado Scrambles: A Guide to 50 Select Climbs in Colorado's Mountains*, and writes the Trail Mix column for *The Denver Post*.

INDEX